Noble Sentiments for an Exile

Noble Sentiments for an Exile

and Other Writings

∽

STEPHEN PAX LEONARD

RESOURCE *Publications* · Eugene, Oregon

NOBLE SENTIMENTS FOR AN EXILE
And Other Writings

Resource Publications
An Imprint of Wipf and Stock Publishers
199 W. 8th Ave., Suite 3
Eugene, OR 97401

www.wipfandstock.com

PAPERBACK ISBN: 979-8-3852-3445-5
HARDCOVER ISBN: 979-8-3852-3446-2
EBOOK ISBN: 979-8-3852-3447-9

For Stan, in memoriam (2017–2024)

Just as I finished writing this book, my beloved spaniel, Stan, was tragically killed. He joined me on many of the journeys that form the backbone of this book. He was the greatest of dogs, the best of companions and will be forever sorely missed.

Contents

CONTENTS

A Bit of Context

'If you rush through life, you see the end-goal in the distance, but you miss the flowers on the way': a Chinese proverb

AT THE HEART OF this short collection of stories, vignettes and travelogues is the appeal of the North (even if occasionally I veer off to more southern climes). Through a variety of encounters in the wildest and most raw parts of northern Europe (but also its cities), it hints at why I am always drawn back to this part of the world, and why these places have exerted such a particular power over me for so long. The appeal lies in the fascination with the landscape, the languages, voices and their sounds, as well as the poetic memory that lives on through my acoustic experience of these places. Some of these journeys began with a voice. I used to listen to short wave radio. Fiddling with the dial, I was constantly intrigued by the crackling, whistling foreign sounds and voices of distant radio stations. I would hover the pin over the peeling labels on the radio set: Leningrad, Riga, Stockholm etc. Only many years subsequently would I go in search of the places behind the voices. Life is in the details, and the stories collected here comprise perhaps a search for that detail – acoustic or otherwise. These vignettes – the results of some of my compulsive wandering – leave me (and my fictional characters) falling in love with the world and everything in it. Such journeys made me think the world was even greater than I had ever fancied. Often, my characters love though a world that is slipping from our grasp – many of these stories embrace a nostalgia and seek to help us escape from the world of time.

My journey takes me down Swedish logging tracks to a rural Sweden that most Swedes have never seen, to near-abandoned Faroese islands in the middle of the Atlantic where I spent the best part of a year. Another year was spent in north-west Greenland. On one of the many journeys in the Polar North, I traveled across the sea ice with a team of sled dogs to a remote, uninhabited island (Northumberland Island). In the manner of a flat-earther, I went in search of the ice edge, and perhaps the boundaries of the human psyche in that frozen world of the High Arctic. Wherever I went, I stood slightly apart from language, be it the language of the Faroese farmer, the Swedish logger, the Russian priest or the Greenlandic narwhal hunter. I like the everyday historicity of the Faroese farmer and the Swedish logger. They use words according to specific circumstances agreed upon by centuries of ancestors. Otherwise, they just stay *schtum*.

Throughout my travels, I sought places that make you look at yourself, and whose beauty makes you feel alive. For some of the people I met on the way, such as those living on remote Faroese islands, going nowhere might result in them coming closer to their senses. On this sensual journey, I ended up longing for this nowhere. Many of the people I met in the Faroes were the embodiment of the old Norse ideals: as well as men of action, they were satirical poets or men of letters. These farmers, shepherds and laborers found freedom in the stillness of the world. A farmer I met in a remote part of Sweden told me that what he liked about the village where he grew up and had lived in his entire life was 'the silence and the smell of the air'.

This phenomenological wandering then took me across the Baltics to Russia, a country famous for its introspection. I traveled on Russian night trains with Stan, my spaniel, in tow. Russia resulted also in an aural awakening for it was here (as well as Ukraine and Romania) where I was seduced by the soft whispery voices in their devout and extraordinary places of worship. I grew to love the sincerity of the Russian people; the manner in which they are grounded in life through their faith and bonds of kinship. I still remember now the first time I attended the All-Night Vigil at Orthodox Christmas; a service that absorbed my whole being and that offered glimpses of the transcendental. I recall standing in the packed church. At midnight, the young, beautiful woman stood in front of me turned her head. Tears were pouring down her face. Somebody once told me if they had to describe sunlight to a blind person, they would have them listen to the Russian Orthodox chants that embody such occasions.

The book opens with *Noble Sentiments for an Exile*, a lyrical essay that charts the anonymous traveler's quest to animate the soundscape of words' inner forms. His extensive travels show him a corporeal world that has been dissolved in the primacy of sound and a sacred that can be grasped through a liberation of the senses. The senses *are* the transcendent principle. For the traveler, the sensuous and the sacred can end up creating a montage of mimetically interwoven voices that make up speech and offer up a pre-modern subjectivity. The traveler seeks these spiritual foundations of language, the poetics of insight and the continuity between the Self and the word. In his dreamy world, speech itself becomes a liturgical act. It is a chant. The experience of speech and exile appear as sub-themes in some of the short travel stories that follow.

As well as this lyrical essay and first person travel accounts, this collection also includes a handful works of semi-fiction which display perhaps more poignantly the shades of my imagination. As the reader will no doubt see, the vectors are not always linear with more ambitious stories sitting alongside simpler tales.

S.P.L.

Credits

Rev'd Dr. Stephen Plant; Gudmund Mortensen; May Britt Skoradal; Poul Ják-up Thomsen; Einar Larsen; Dr. Cosima Gillhammer; Peter Harris; Kathryn Wallace; Rev'd Hugh Wybrew; Ilze Saleniece; David Qujaukitsoq; Ana-Sofia Imiina; the babushka in St Petersburg who delivered a lecture in the most forthright of manners to the train guard that had refused to let me and Stan on the train, explaining that I was 'a foreigner with a friendly dog'. She won; the train guard lost.

OTHER APPEARANCES

Clutag Press, Little Toller Books and Elsewhere (A journal of place) allowed me to reproduce versions of previously published material, either online or in print format. Grateful acknowledgement to their editors.

'Voices, voices. Listen, my heart, the way only saints have listened till now' (Rainer Maria Rilke)

Noble Sentiments for an Exile

A lyrical essay

Psalm 121 (The Traveler's Psalm)

I lift up my eyes to the mountains—
Where does my help come from?
My help comes from the Lord,
The Maker of heaven and earth.
He will not let your foot slip—
He who watches over you will not slumber;
Indeed, he who watches over Israel
Will neither slumber nor sleep.
The Lord watches over you—
The Lord is your shade at your right hand;
The sun will not harm you by day,
Nor the moon by night.
The Lord will keep you from all harm—
He will watch over your life;
The Lord will watch over your coming and going
Both now and forevermore

THE TRAVELER WAS ONCE told that language is the bridge between the material world and the intimate life tied up in our souls. Continuous with essence, language should make this inner world accessible, he had heard. He imagined an inner spirit that can still locate this forgotten traditional cosmos to be one comprising fleeting visions of wild places that occasionally resurface in one's memory – bewildering exteriority, fragments of poetry and whispers of the sacred. The sacred and the profane, the public and the private, the extraordinary and the mundane – sometimes it is at such experiential junctions where the force of language can still be felt. These were the kind of accounts that he had heard on his journeys.

He was also told that when we discover the sacred, we hear words that are still *alive*, not disfigured and frozen. Listening to the sounds of these words, we in turn feel *alive* as their different sounds and impressions reverberate within us in unique ways. The traveler cannot escape these sensations. They become material and are sensuously perceived. At this point, language no longer acts as a referential vehicle and that is all well and good. Conventions can then be swept aside and new paradigms embraced. It is time for the sensuous or so the traveler believed. However, the traveler understood that language only really comes alive in voice for it is through sound that language becomes external. Speech is an alive entity through the endless permutations of voice giving order to all that breath. In those 'scriptural societies' laden with logocentrism that the traveler sought to leave behind, voices can become lost and spoken words that span centuries can be misplaced. The solitary pilgrimages to the almost abandoned monasteries that leave him overwhelmed by the voices of the world are neglected.

There are though still paths that show the traveler what it is like when voice is free from its systemic and societal shackles, when it is 'decolonized' (but not in the political sense of the word) in our bountiful dreams. When a long-lost friend says 'it is me', the sound of the voice conquers the generality of the pronoun – an ontological horizon is disclosed by the voice. The voice subjectivizes the person who emitted the sound and tells us everything about his character: overbearing or shy; humble or supercilious; benevolent or cruel. And when there is only a voice and it is amplified in the near-silence of the night, the traveler's verbal consciousness is electrified. A door to another realm stands ajar. Wishing to push the door open and enter the palace of transcendence, the traveler keeps wandering until he uncovers the spiritual speech acts and the intrinsic dignity of language. This journey offers exceptional possibility.

If the traveler is fully awake in speech, and is directed to places where perception and expression converge, speaking and the *Lebenswelt* can then be intertwined. And so, he steps out of the language shadow. Then, the traveler traces the essence of consciousness, and he follows the paths where the voices echo in his dreams – that is his perennial quarry. Oh, the life of the mind! Despite societies defining and redefining themselves *without* this voice – the signifier of the Christian spirit – the traveler still makes language of course. He is constantly restyling it but he no longer listens to it. Discourse has been sanitized and the tongue is no longer sanctified by words alone. The meanings of words have been exhausted and humanity has fallen into a collective inertia.

The language the traveler loves has little communicative value. Its appeal is acoustic and sensorial but seldom semantic. Every traveler knows that language enjoys its greatest impact when it is still a chain of sensory representations, but these moments are typically fleeting and ephemeral. Focus on the meaning and the aesthetic appeal of words is mislaid in the cool reality of the shadows. When the sounds become meaningful, attention to the voice is often distracted and deprioritized. The pleasure afforded by the words of languages and their component sounds can be sensual, but it is the voice that is the signifier of re-enchantment. Re-enchantment, that was surely the traveler's quest? The boundaries of the impossible.

From all the conversations he had overheard in crowded train carriages and noisy bazaars, the traveler knew, however, that this re-enchantment and creativity is lost as soon as he opens his mouth. All that every day speech was heteronomous and was influenced by forces beyond the individual. The words fall out of his mouth without him having to consciously shape and organize them. He wanted to ungag himself from the words already spoken. The traveler was anxious not to lose sight of the inner form of language – the chain of sensory impressions that inform the memory and perhaps even the soul –, for then poetry would become prose. He wanted to hear the voice of the word. He could hear the working of the spirit in those monosyllabic words such as 'God' and 'love' sing to him. It is the consciousness of this inner form that makes words 'poetry', a shepherd who traveled with the wind once told him. The inner form is what makes the content. When the word loses its inner form or when the inner form no longer suggests itself to the speaker or listener, the word loses its symbolic meaning. It turns into a concept, just a plain old concept that doesn't know the oblique life.

Despite the prosaic nature of speech, the traveler continued to create himself not just through his own vocal and linguistic tapestries subconsciously crafted over the course of generations, but also through conscious word-selection. The words he spoke were not ideographic 'blank slates', but had long and complicated 'social histories' of usage being passed from speaker to speaker, community to community, and embedded the tiniest of cultural connotations. As living entities, all these words have a life, a journey and stories to tell too. Their meanings can change dramatically over time before they eventually die or transform into a new coinage. The traveler also understood that words don't have fixed meanings. Not only do they change over time, their meanings shift in subtle ways when juxtaposed with other words.

For the traveler that knows the desert and the caravan routes, there might also be the appeal of the obsolete, a retreat to the archaic: a word that is very seldom heard brings with it some kind of auditory sensation. Just listen to the camel drivers. They speak and the inheritance of these words and idioms flows forth. And a voice is not just noise; it is a phenomenological presence. What is more, the voice is transcendental. It transcends the body like some kind of sonic shadow. The traveler knows better than most that in order to feel a sense of being at home, there requires a journey of homecoming and that itself can too be transcendental. Just go to a railway station and look at the faces of all the people that have been some-place else.

* * *

And the traveler had also heard about sacred languages and the canonical books. If there is a language of Gods and a language of Men, then there is also the sacred liturgical language which acts as a conduit between the two. The sacred language branches off into the distant past through the cathedrals of the traveler's mind. The traveler who is at home in distant places as well as distant times chooses the mystical interiority of language and the forgotten monasteries where obedience is measured in terms of renunciation, not the dust and sweat of the city where people like to own things. On the road, the traveler's senses are wide open and his creative memory becomes his epic faculty. He wants to chronicle all that that floats past him. The way his body absorbs language is part of this memory. Here, the traveler can escape the Heideggerian *Gerede* ('idle talk') chained to its banal shadows and return to the physicality of the word; the kinship of language *is* the traveler's motto after all. The traveler understands that language can transcend the register of its causative operations when its sounds scatter throughout his body. He likes to push language to its limits and for him this feeling has a quality of nobility.

'Object to any instrumentalist concept of language', a blind Bedouin scholar had once told the traveler. He could still hear those words being mumbled in the corner of his mind. Language should linger in the memory;

it is more than expression in the form of words. More than a means of verbalizing all those rationalities that belong to no one. With the lore of the past, the traveler is looking instead for words that feel like the echo of the soul or for the nostalgia that perhaps never was. The traveler had trespassed across these word shadows and stumbled across ancient liturgical languages such as Church Slavonic – an incorruptible language, frozen in time that has never really had a life beyond the temple, this sanctuary of echoes where sounds are spaced differently. Modernizers tried to tweak the language, committing acts of heresy but the traveler sought to embrace all that perceived immutability. With such idioms and all their verbal somersaults and encrypted syntax, the traveler speculated whether there might be a hope of reaching a higher level, some kind of transcendental realm – transcendental perhaps because it is always just out of the traveler's reach but nonetheless dances along reality's substratum. What kind of journey would enable the spiritual to acquire a mastery over the material? A journey where the traveler can break out of the prison of his own circular feelings and motions, and where the castle doesn't sink in the sand.

With an ear to the ancient, a liturgical language seems to have some kind of existence *ab aeterno*. He is not talking about mystical exaltation or yesterday's axioms, but is mourning a language almost gone. The postscripts of the broken; a set of sensations, some kind of verbal *tableaux vivants*. He could see the beauty in what is vanishing; the electricity of all those vibrations that ran through his body. We enjoy these treasures so briefly. Everything is almost obsolete. And so, his journey was a pilgrimage into the far boundaries of speech, the potency of language, the world of silence, the dialectical tongue, a journey to escape the promiscuity of words and actions, a wandering to the places where the fabrics that bind the worshipper to his past can be seen. Silence, or you can call it systems of signification, if you like. The traveler could find peace in this kind of opulent silence, the silence that emerges from the pitter-patter of rain.

The traveler's language is also the locus of his infinite private world, and these private worlds communicate most intensively during the pensive hours when he takes himself to the places he knows least about. The world of sound is indeed a private world. The traveler would surround himself by greater and lesser persons, but the sounds bouncing around in the traveler's head and penetrating his body could only be his. This jumble of sentences and itineraries, that array of proverbial virtues. His inner monologues mean that few can really know how he thinks.

The traveler had observed how language can grow organically out of nature and create a miasma of semiotic confusion for those who like rules and conventions. He could see how language was more than a symbolic representation; his travels through a hundred lands had taught him how it is interwoven into our *Lebenswelt* and negotiates the dialectic between language and experience. Words don't just describe a pre-existing thing, but can actually be that thing. And experience is passed from mouth to mouth. These words and morphemes have their own inner lives and the speaker's linguistic intuition and appreciation of these autochthonous forms should be sensuous, or at least that was the traveler's view.

The weary traveler negotiates the shady area between the intelligible and the non-intelligible, and this is sometimes the locus for the most sensuous language – the flame of life. When the traveler cannot quite grasp the meaning, the non-semantic features of the language, perhaps certain paralinguistic features or the stress, rhythm, and intonation patterns become perceptually more prominent. In these shady areas, the traveler seeks to embrace the words that have gone before him. And what are these words? They are incarnate sensualities. Is it such sensualities that draws the traveler to the counsel of the Orthodox liturgy in Russia? Or is it the peculiar attitude to the image that Russia inherited from Byzantium?

He had come to a city of golden domes and bronze statues. His head is full of words. Under squadrons of clouds and on streets lined with golden maples drugged by autumn, he walks towards his rejoicing conscience with mutilated memory. Closes the door of the church and shuts out the vexations of the ordinary world. The miracle of time having stood still. It was the traveler who always sought to eke out these ancient places of worship – probably hoping for a little resacralization, but also always happy to sidestep any *aggiornamento*. The traveler was never modern. And the traveler wasn't just going from place-to-place; no, this was moreover an interior journey to make straight his paths. A sort of spiritual connecting the dots in that world of incorporeal desires as he sought to be adorned with grace and catch a glimmer of salvation. He didn't seek an intellectual experience. He wanted though to be in covenant with God and at the heart of his contemplative journey was a dialogue with God, and so he sought out places where he could sprawl out his soul.

Stand amongst the anointed pilgrims cowled in headscarves – their abstention is noble and lofty, he liked to remind himself. They are the servants of God and wait humbly upon the Lord's will. Their souls progress in sanctity. Tied with the fetters of human affairs, when the traveler comes here he is attracted to what lies above. The incense drifts across the temple and the sound of the priest's voice becomes even more penetrating as one of his senses becomes obscured. The words ricochet off the ascetic walls of the palace of believers. The concealed voices from behind the iconostasis acquire features of an autonomous object. Philology pours forth, organizing all the immutable morality. Deacons stumble over ciphered words in ancient books. The traveler's consciousness strays. He is reminded of his imperfections. The link between voice and subjectivity is severed and he is left searching for the interiority of words. Once the voice is apparently detached from the body, it assumes a special authority. It is as if language has an independent existence, as if the words are descending from the heavens.

The traveler sought to embrace this ambiguity for he thought this explained why chanting was so alluring. He warmed to its liminality, its inbetweenness, the fact that it is neither quite singing nor talking. How can the traveler conquer the unknown? The repeated words; the vibrating substrata. The psalmody is fruit for the soul. Chanting was for the traveler a kind of spiritual agency, a means of divine rapprochement. What are the associations of a chanting voice that is always testing the boundaries between speech and music, the traveler wondered? The sounding and the resounding, the blurring of cause and effect, the Byzantine vocalization of the sacred that somehow forms a moment of existence. A sense of timelessness as the traveler waits for the sage to appear. A reminder that language is always chasing reality; a reminder to the traveler that we still don't understand the impact of language on our spiritual estate.

With chanting there is a sense that God hovers above the creation of words for he breathes life into man. The traveler went looking for God, looking for signification or at least another dimension of being. He was hoping to find a language, an erudition of sensuousness or a way of speaking that would show him a transcendental realm. He fancied a spiritual (or liturgical) language can direct the believer towards a spiritual consciousness, some kind of sublime detachment. He followed the paths of ritual language that led to a heightened poetic function for it told the traveler the circumstances under which God must be present. It is ritual that shapes poetics and inspires devotion, or so the traveler thought. A sacred language might appear as the embodiment of God; the *almost* accessible words are reimagined in inner speech, enabling both a physical and psychological interiority that constantly manifests itself as a presence. The distinctiveness of a language can be reflected in the relative authority of its words, and a sacred language can show the traveler another world and if he is really lucky another dimension entirely. Vaguely aware of this, the traveler fumbles in the dark, looking for words that might index divinity.

The priest's voice opens up a field of sublimated meanings and has the potential to grasp the listener corporeally. 'Put aside the western rationalism, and let the mysteries of God wash over you', a toiler of fields whispers in the traveler's ear. Then, words can become sounds again. 'Orthodox ontologies don't focus on a dichotomy of inner spirit and outward material forms...no, no...', the voice continued and so words really were free to occupy a liminal, existential space. The traveler had witnessed how in Orthodoxy belief systems have been sustained in words and customs, and not devalued. He could see how little had been spoilt by the stains of history. Here, the traveler can still find an experience that maps out the common faith, he reckoned. Here the traveler is reminded that God *is* a mystery.

The traveler likes to escape from the oceanic rubble of the ordinary and return to those places where the sounds of words confer their allegorical power, where he can find life in its fullness. He aims to leave behind trivial things on his path. He has left behind the trash of modernity and searches for the impossible amidst the forgotten lands where they still harvest frankincense and myrrh. Shadows fly past him. He understands how the profusion of things has conspired to conceal the erosion of belief systems and the scarcity of ideas. To break from the silent procession of the days, he takes himself to the nowheres where the relationship between form and meaning is symbiotic as well as semiotic. He wants to rediscover the living force of words for when words become dissociated from life, life itself is lessened. Words of others just in the end become a voice and a potential shipwreck of misunderstandings.

The traveler, however, felt the need for words and so he actively eked out those moments of heightened linguistic consciousness such as the context of language learning or listening to a sacred language in a church – those places colored by the mute silences of memory. Only memory allows for possibility. It is in these places where a curious worshipper reduces speech to its elementary level of phenomenological factors and that in turn gives him a particular articulation of the conceptual understanding of language. He wants to jump from the signified to the signifier. He is looking for the essence of the prayer; the *real* custodian of the word but can words alone conquer the spirits?

On flight and exile, and by dint of a little elaborate auditory imagination, the traveler thought he could find a new spiritual reality that is empowering. If a traveler becomes an exile, his displacement will mold him for he can (if he wishes) become part of a new reality. A new reality because he has become a fugitive from the material world and his observations are fashioned from new and different ways of speaking. Only once set apart, can the traveler – a lover of simplicity – begin to understand things. Surely, all travelers harbor dreams of exile. Exile *is* the Christian story.

Focusing on voice, the traveler in his spiritual wanderings might want to access the structures of immediacy and the ontology of an acoustic presence. The first few syllables of a familiar voice can convey a whole gamut of memories, emotions, associations and opinions. A familiar voice on one of those perilous passageways can trigger an experiential vision. Spoken words are translated into life and the voice is absolutely key to this transition, as every traveler knew. If the same words were uttered by a completely unfamiliar voice, the impact might be non-existent or at least the same vision of life would not have been generated. It is the voice that brings about the presence of the speaker – be it the herder, the priest, the hermit or the inner-city vagrant. It is the associations that bring a word to life, but these associations can be magnified and enriched if the word is spoken with a voice that is appealing to the traveler. The word has an acoustic appeal too, but the voice can either detract from or embellish the appeal.

The traveler's observations about language are most acute when his knowledge of the relevant idiom is incomplete, when his fallible ear hears things that mean other things. Then, he still has the privilege of being in touch with his acoustic intuitions vis-à-vis voice and the musicality of language. The familiarity of voice and language deadens his senses and the texture of his experiences. Once fluency is gained, the traveler's experience of language becomes gradually presupposed. The sense of linguistic and acoustic wonder is lost. It is the phenomenological equivalent of a child becoming an adult. Bit-by-bit, he loses his naïveté. When the traveler is *within* language, he stands apart from the horizons of sound. He is focused on the semantic meaning. However, when he stands slightly apart from language (perhaps because of an imperfect understanding of the language or because the voice is unfamiliar), his focus drifts occasionally to the features that comprise the resonance of voice. The traveler spent years placing words, bits of words and phrases in the cells of the mind's honeycomb. Always in the midst of those that spoke a foreign idiom, he was captivated by the sounds of words again and understood that not only the inner character of the speaker but the sense of place and the deep structure of the sensory landscape emanates from those words. And the meaning, the true meaning, well, that is to be found at the top of a spiral staircase.

As well as vocal pastiches, the traveler creates his own idiolect, his own linguistic personality. But these idiolects are not created *ex nihilo*: language is always contiguous on language. The traveler thinks of language as a primal activity of self-creation and speech is the process of self-identification through thinking, but all the time he knows he is weaving other peoples' words, expressions and voices into his own linguistic tapestry. This is an ongoing, habitual practice. Familiar voices, words, turns of phrase become potentially exposures of being – the utterance of an unusual turn of phrase unique to that person brings that person alive. A certain expression can be inseparable from its speaker. Linguistic signs can be inseparable from what makes them meaningful.

Through voice, forms of words can be psychosomatically integrated into their meaning. The word 'God' can be part of the idea of 'God'. And for a word not to become stale, there should be a tangible meaning in the sound. Let the traveler not forget, the voice precedes, but also succeeds language. The traveler has a voice before he can articulate words, and once the words are forgotten the sound of the voice echoes in his mind. It may be difficult for the traveler to separate voice and words, but he can experience voice before he can understand the meaning of the words. At this point in his life, he is experiencing voice at its level of musicality.

On an exquisite afternoon of introspection in one of those unremembered seasons, the traveler pondered how it is only once words are written down, does language become like a musical notation. First (if the language is unfamiliar), there is just music. Subsequently, it has this objectified second life, but the traveler had overlooked this. In this second life, language acts as if it controls the invisible, but in actual fact the invisible is controlling the reality and the experience of the perception. The traveler embraces this new language as if it is a magnificent flirt with the spirit of humanity. He loved to yield to these desires. With a new language in his palms, the traveler grows young again. Language turns on the sensuous codes in the traveler's brain when he only partially understands it. He grasps for the meaning, but his or her ear receives part semantic meaning, part music. Through endless repetition and use, the strangeness of a new linguistic form soon dissipates and seeps into the world of signification. Then, his relationship to language and voice changes completely. When the voice or language is new and unfamiliar, it offers an immediacy and dynamism. Learning a new language, the traveler is confronted with new linguistic forms all the time and appreciates signs in a broader symbolic context. Signs also represent a transcendent reality and help the traveler cross frontiers. The traveler knows, however, that language never gives just a taxonomy of signs and the traveler seldom commands a clear view of the use of these signs.

Absorbed by the revolving world, the traveler would create his own contingent reality based purely on the sounds that he heard on his journeys. He was always looking for a voice that could turn on these sensuous codes and make the pursuit of virtue sweeter; the splicing of the inner and outer consciousness. Who doesn't love to dwell in this schizophonia and convince themselves of the legitimacy of pleasure?, he thought to himself. Who doesn't seek the acme of mystical experience? The traveler too knew the swoonings of love. With all those voices from nowhere appealing to the sincerity of his senses, the traveler felt as if he was riding a thermal of abstraction – so happy in this world, this sum of wonders. Outside, there is the ordinary world. The same muffled voices, the same indistinct figures that float past, but in his inner world he was playing hide and seek with the shadows in the garden. At moments like this, the world was to the traveler an intoxicating joy. It was the possession of these languages that gave him the right to decide his fate.

The traveler's Ulyssean peregrinations traversing a variety of experiential sensations turned from weeks to months. His wandering took him across cities growing each year like tree trunks and swollen by hierarchies, through forests, across moors, up and down valleys, through cities decimated by pandemics, over mountain tops and through mosquito infested swamps. He never tired of the freedom – the dominion of the possible – that travel brought him. As he traveled, it became clearer to him that the world was chockablock with referents whose meaning had been misplaced. For example, some of the peoples he met along the way had lost their faith in God or indeed in the gods; their biographies had been blown away. And how can someone who only knows a material life understand what a soul is anyway?

The voice calls each day upon the people that make up the nations of the world. It just depends on them whether they heed that inner call or not.

Having zig-zagged the continents, the traveler returned, baptized by the beauty of that world, to that special, quiet place, to the sweetness of exile and that lost idea that you can create your own world entirely *ab initio*. The sabbath of the memory. Everything seemed as if it had always been known – and yet it was just a new beginning. He was no longer beyond the world, but could hear the testimony of the pious and was full of gratitude. He was happy in all things; seasoned by the hope of what is to become. The eve of ever greater graces seemed nigh. The chaffs of his deeds had been mercifully blown away and storms no longer kindled in the traveler's limbs. He dwelt in stillness. Canticles were being sung in a distant land. He might have returned home, left behind skies that afflicted the traveler's soul, the places where people speak so much they don't even understand the truths they reveal, but he understood very well that the road continues, on and on. This is the spiritual way. And soon, he would prepare for new beginnings; longing again for the unbeaten track.

It was time to rest.

The traveler closed his eyes, arresting the sequence of years, and felt the shape of his soul in the words that he uttered. He inhaled the transcendent grace and was in communion with the true light. He felt as noble as those blessed ones who had departed but stood around listening. A flicker of consciousness and sleep descended on the traveler. He passed through centuries of civilization and citadels of clay. Everywhere he went he met people with songs of praise on their lips. They spoke arcane dialects of love and endowed their words with compassion. Their voices were velvety and hung in the wind, giving them a divine like quality. The soft whisperings of the traveler's dreams could be heard everywhere.

Chapter 1: Russia

'Love is short, forgetting is long' (Pablo Neruda)

Hotel d'Angleterre

An enigmatic encounter in St Petersburg

THE AMERICAN MET HER in the Hotel d'Angleterre in the middle of one of those endless Russian winters. She told him the hotel had become well-known because a famous Russian poet had died – perhaps committed suicide – in one of the rooms. They met a few years ago, but even now he still remembered her pale blue Siberian eyes, her flaxen hair. She was always *très parfumé*. Then there was her voice, her language and all those other bits that do not quite reach the definition of language. Her soft voice bespoke a tumultuous sensuality. Sometimes, it became heavy, transmitting the decades of repression that defined this country still pondering its Soviet past and lost poets. Her voice was made for a cantata of untold epics, her discourse was one of metaphysical barriers that flirted with a spiritual world. Her utterances were simple and human, articulated in the voices of her forebears. Those long sighs of hers conveyed that Russian substratum of pessimism, he supposed, but he was enchanted by her carefully chosen words that described a country choked on its history. She would cast him a glance and pepper her speech with Pushkinesque epigrams: 'there is no happiness in the world. Only peace and freedom'. This kind of thing. He wanted to know more. He wanted to peel away some of those layers of enigma.

And so, they walked the streets of St Petersburg beneath cupolas that glittered in the reddish light of the low sun. Then the sky disappeared and the cold imprisoned their words. She walked angularly and with refined elegance. In sub-zero temperatures, they went from museum to church to café, warming up intermittently over cups of steaming tea. In the churches, he had followed her eyes, the sacred dreams that filled her gaze, and was subsequently chastised for doing so. In the cafés, he let his gaze take in the room. Elderly couples married for scores of years lapped *borscht* from heavy soup spoons. They whispered and exchanged spasmodic sighs. Even their breathing was coordinated. They kept saying the same thing over and over again – their lives were on repeat. Their phrases symbolized the absurdity of their lives. When they spoke, they barely moved their lips. The words lost their borders entirely. They were so used to one another's voices and empty talk that they could no longer hear one another. Their talk was just familiar, patterned noise. Their hands began to assume fixed latitudes; their moods were perfectly intertwined. They lived slowly. They wore maudlin expressions. Waitresses would occasionally interrupt their sparse conversation. Armed with dessert trolleys overflowing with cheese cake, these aproned women bumped into one another and burst into a hurricane of language. On the adjacent table sat a woman, ridden with anxiety. The toing and froing of guests irked her. The American watched the woman eat. She ate too fast. The fork entered her mouth too violently. She fondled nervously the cutlery and moved the condiments around the table as if they were chess pieces.

Their breaks at these cafés were typically brief during these short days. Once they had decoded one another's questions, they moved on wending their way through a curious juxtaposition of dehumanizing Lego of Kruschchyovka, obelisks, Byzantine glory, stucco candy-floss and magnificent Baroque churches. They passed through gilded palaces, admired ecstasies of art and next to her, his imagination surged, trespassing the corners of his mind. Their voices stung by the cold, they spoke in half-sentences and facial expressions that froze like grinning statues. There was a pattern of silences-questions-reflections. When she asked a question, she would fix him with her pale blue eyes in an interrogatory manner. Everything about her was mysterious. She would wear a distant air of philosophical seclusion. She was delicate and indescribable. There was a certain coldness too, but no guile. Occasionally, there would be a hint of her fiery mettle. Something in her would burst forth, but then she would soon return to talking about more mundane practicalities.

The appeal of these encounters had never left him. They invested their words with a sense of trust that was perhaps misplaced. The lack of agreement on the shared meaning of words left the cultural deficit being made up through other means. Like a mental refugee devoid of native glibness, he spoke using defective words. He spoke in unambiguous idioms, avoiding the temptation of obsolete turns of phrase. The language gap filled in the gaps that might exist between two speakers of the same language. They repeated disconnected words. There were times when her words were more sound than meaning, allowing him to ponder their poetry. Much of the time was spent engineering elaborate paraphrases to explain what they meant in maximally simple terms whilst they navigated their way through a tapestry of cultural faux-pas. There was never space for platitudes. The questions were never sterile. Finding a consensus in such a context meant twice as much as in a monolingual situation. An agreement was met with a knowing smile of mutual recognition and a sense of relief that the ill-declined words were no longer needed. Occasionally, there was a meeting of eyes in broken conversation, an enigmatic glance that seemed to say 'we trusted our fate'.

He only really found the lost expressions once he took her to the Mariinsky Theatre. Her eyes feasted on the choreographic splendor, and he discerned a little hope that she would unravel before him. Her emotions started to decant; a grin fleeted across her cheeks. Stern-faced women with crimson lips and priggish frowns appeared from carriages in cloud-lets of exclamation under a darkled sky. December had marched across the city. Inside the theatre, the atmosphere was Soviet. Provident women, as tough as tank drivers, punched orders to maidens in the cloakroom. Young unsmiling, amorous couples were being photographed in curtained alcoves. Everywhere he looked, men and women were parading in their finery, trading pleasantries with thin lips and perusing their figures in the looking-glass.

In the stalls, she sunk into the softness of the scarlet velvet seats, and there was suddenly a tinge of emotion, a glow of passion as she steadied herself for the sumptuousness of *The Nutcracker*. Her long, slender fingers occasionally groped for his. Her occasional words took on a bodily meaning. A Russian ballet of silver houses and Marmalade castles had been a sensible choice. The music would fill their communicative gaps as he tried to conceal his boredom having suffered enough ballets. She was in awe of the gravity defying moves. Tender girls crossed the stage in gliding *bourrées*; lines of weightless dancers hopped with implacable rhythm; nymphs floated insubstantially in the arms of men. She sighed at the weighty incantation of the dance, and sat in awe of the *Trepak*. The ballet reached its festive apotheosis, and the audience burst into rapturous applause. It was almost Christmas time.

They leave the clamor of the post-performance theatre, and walk in the hushed streets thick with snow amidst the broken-up moonlight. They exchange brief, staccato commentaries on the performance. Consonants stick in clouds of frozen breath and her unstressed vowels are low in energy. She grips his arm tightly as if her life were in danger, 'cold, cold', she says. They side-step *matryoshka* doll vendors and stop at a church a few compact streets away to find some warmth and hear the church poetry roll forth. He closes the door firmly behind them and blocks out the world.

Inside, they are treated to the glorious solemnity of vespers: profoundly meditative in its warm religiosity. They stand, engulfed in the laws of harmony. The chanting, the whispers, the voices cascading off the stone walls unify in a divine consonance, an unforced congruence. The church is packed with cartels of genuflecting women wearing languid brows, semicircling in front of the altar. A beggar files between them, and is cast scornful glances. Almost symphonically, the despair is soon counterpointed with hope. The priest chants the doxology in a ritualized fashion, barely pausing for breath. There are no pulpits here. In this house of enigma, schizophrenically both Christian and non-Western, part church, part picture gallery, the sense of wonder and estrangement is still alive. Like a Scriabin symphonic poem, the icons imply another world. A world that triggers the sensibilities in a mysterious and intuitive manner, suspending the worshipper in some kind of hyperreal realm where thoughts can skid and scatter in a thousand directions. Scriabin believed spiritual liberation could be attained through the stimulation of these senses and that ultimately we would be replaced by more 'nobler beings'. The American sought to float on these introspective thermals. The Divine Liturgy at an Orthodox Church fits the human soul somehow, he thought to himself. The ritual repetition of liturgy marks some kind of spiritual revival, a spiral of conflated endings and beginnings. The American felt as if he was taken back to an ancient past but at the same time shown a new future. These were the moments that possessed him entirely, the moments that had a perpetual life in his mind. There can be a religious or sacred significance to one single moment, he thought to himself. A single moment of revelation and lives can be suddenly transformed.

As a theologian once told him with a hint of darkness; 'the universe of discourse is lost'. The East and West became strangers. It feels symbolic for their encounter and especially to meet at such a time. They stand in silence, wallowing in the antitheses of the Orthodox chants. The priest sings with an innate mournfulness. People gather around, brought together by a subjective experience of an invisible presence. Writing is no longer privileged over orality. The American wonders what all this means for her, whether they can share some intimacies too and know a little something they didn't know before. He had always been egged on by these apparently unbridgeable gaps. If he were lucky, she might flash him a smile, and he would feel satisfied for having transgressed the opaque gaze. In his more optimistic moments, he sometimes felt he spotted a lascivious wink, but he might have been dreaming. After an hour or so of shifting laboriously weight from one leg to another, the worshippers spill out from this holiness onto the muffled stillness of the fresh snow. Her breath pours forward in billowing cumulus like a steaming kettle and freezes on his face. Soft snow falls vertically. Outside the church, post-Soviet *babushkas* wrapped in countless layers beg and seek a merciful God. Their faces are spangled with white stars. The couple's contemplative footsteps scrunch in the snow. The streetlamp lights up her glass-cutting cheek bones, manicured eyelashes and pursed lips. Chained to his helping arm, he places her on the protected side of the pavement, steering her away from the curb to ensure she is not splashed with unpleasantness or *kasha* ('porridge') as they call it here. He listens to her intently. She excites his heart for her love cannot be won. It was always muted somehow. It was masochism perhaps, but he felt the vines of his heart become tangled. He knew she would never be his, and that there would never be any blandishments on offer. He knew well the tyranny of the passions.

He guides her past frozen canals, through the labyrinthine streets of Tsarist Russia under the beam of the moonlight. They dissect parks where poets used to duel amongst battalions of nude statues. Snowdrifts grope the windowsills of empty palaces decorated with Repin, Shishkin, Makovsky and Kandinsky. Traffic herds in the boulevards, waiting to cross the hundreds of bridges that speak in Dostoyevskian metaphors of nineteenth century struggles. The mundane is just a few steps away. Beneath, the pancake ice of the Neva creaks and groans. Along its embankments, this city of sinister dreamers spreads itself out generously. The pink-façaded palaces where the cream of St. Petersburg society danced *mazurkas* have almost vanished into the evening sky.

Back at the Hotel d'Angleterre, Mussorgsky spiraled out of the radio. The piano throbbed and inconsolable longing suffused every word that poured forth from the lyrical song. The piece closes with a fateful timpani roll. Locks of blonde hair frame her ivory forehead. The green-shaded banker's lamp lights her brow; the soft gleam spreading to her clavicle. Her sharp elbows dig into the *manchettes* of the armchair. Her long, elongated hands are spread out on the velvet upholstery. She lay supine. Her long, slender legs dangled over the ottoman. He listens to her whispery coil of words; regimes of slippery sibilants sliding into one another. He did not want her to stop speaking. Listening to her was a warm, embracing sensation, like a mother grasping a child on the threshold of a doorstep after a time apart. He listened to the way she placed the words together, tracing their curvaceous cadences. The quirks of the language; the bruising, on-off journey he had been on with this language spanning many years. Russian. She was always a difficult lover. There could be no doubt.

He wants her to talk about Omsk. That vast Siberian landmass just floated in his memory. Like most foreigners, he could not quite imagine those industrial cities whose names imparted so little. Tomsk, Omsk, Tobolsk. Unsurprisingly, she does not share his curiosity. She shrugs her shoulders: 'cold city, you know. Not much to do there. Theatre, some churches. Not much. Just work'. There is a melancholy in her words. Through the indexical footprints of voice, she creates herself. He could feel the years rolling by when she spoke about the city. He knew there must be more. It is not so much the place that interests him, but the people. The children of the intellectuals that survived the gulags, sitting in their tiny overheated Krushchyovka flats trying to piece together their difficult histories. Russians had often told him there was no reason to go to these places, but he had to convince himself that they were wrong. 'I don't know', she said. 'Maybe you come to visit'. She then reached for her bag and produced a beautifully wrapped gift. 'Here, this is for you. It is from Omsk'. He caresses the shiny wrapping paper. 'It is a book', he says with a grin. It was the history of the Romanov family. Inside she had written 'Enjoy your time in St Petersburg. It is nice to meet you. Maria.' There were no kisses (x). He asks her why. 'What is this?', she says. 'We not have this'. 'Why would I write this?'. It felt like a Russian explanation. He could feel himself fondling around, looking for scraps of hope in the dark, but there was never more than an occasional smidgin of light. Something ephemeral. Slowly, a heavy fatigue began to girdle her shoulders. She falls silent and drifts into sleep.

In the days that followed, they fought and bickered. Misunderstandings increased and went beyond the threshold expected of any half-decent conversation. Sometimes they resorted to their distinctive languages that would collide and grate. The sheer pleasure of trying to understand was fading. Her speech became jumbled syllables; a thick jungle of words. The silences grew longer as they breakfasted on *vareniki*. They had an afternoon apart. She disappeared to see a Siberian friend and only returned in the quiet of the night. He explored the fringes of the city, looking for hidden churches and he didn't know what. The following morning, he took her to the railway station under a sky of solid white, wishing for a note of reconciliation before she departed. It was a short walk. He carried her case and reached for her hand. Her long fingers were perfectly proportioned.

The concourse was full of stern-faced commuters; shadows flashed past them, heads buried between scarf and *ushanka*. The snowy traces of their itineraries scattered on the floor between the kiosks selling *blini*. There seemed to be much to say, but suddenly there was little time. She grabbed him tight. Her body trembled in the cold. The embrace was short, but firm. 'Please come to Omsk'. Then, she was gone and all his questions were left unanswered. Her slender figure disappeared into the crowd surging up the platform, and the American was alone again in this world with the burden of human consciousness. Desires became memories once again.

The *kvass* seller

A certain kind of longing

SHE LONGED FOR THE sea. She had waited all summer to hear the waves crash on the shore and swim in the bumpy waters. Those were childhood memories for her, the moments of freedom that she cherished by the shores of the Black Sea. She had to dream of something whilst she was stuck in Simferopol. Every day she traveled through the flat country along the pot-holed lanes that weaved their way through sun-baked vineyards to come to the city to sell her wares. The bus was hot and she felt closed in. Tempers frayed each time it stopped and another vendor squeezed his way on the *paziki* as those square-shaped Soviet buses are known. The passengers all faced the sliding windows in the hope of getting some fresh air. The driver punched the horn and cursed at anything that obstructed their path. Behind his cab a sign reminds passengers *lgot net* 'no special rates'. His hands flew from the hot leather steering wheel, flicking away oncoming vehicles. He threatened malefactors with ash from the filterless cigarette that hung from his mouth. The bus would pass sellers of peaches whose fruit were laid out in trays on stalls and organized by size. Then, there were the sweet red onion stalls. The shiny Yalta onions hung like giant beads on strings. As the bus approached the city, the streets became choked with morning traffic. Cars inched around the roundabouts decorated with statues of admirals. Loudspeakers wished the city-dwellers a happy *prazdnik*, Simferopol day, farmers' day, teachers' day or whatever that particular day's celebration might be. There would surely be fireworks tonight.

Once on the main high street, she would get off the bus and trudge up the road until she found an elusive rectangle of shade where she would set up her stall. She had lived her life in these shadows, waiting for an interruption to the near-terminal boredom. The sun was already hot. She stared down at her mobile phone to check the temperature, but the internet flickered and then cut off. She laid out the honey-colored bottles of *kvass* on the stall. Her regular customers soon came, handing over a hundred ruble note and placing the bottle under arm. They would exchange pleasantries and the day dragged on. On the other side of the pavement, a caged bird kept indoors pecked constantly at an apartment window. Even in the shade, the afternoon heat scorched her skin. She looked at her watch frequently. It was to be one of those Fridays where nothing seemed to happen. The velvety notes of the bells began to ring out from the churches where she had nearly married and whose frescos had been recently restored by French and Italian artisans. It was 5pm, and she thought it was perhaps time to take the bus home.

A tall, white-trousered man with a wiry frame and olive skin approached the stall. It was Araz, a friend of her uncle's. 'I hear your *kvass* is good, my dear?' he asks before laughing and giving her a warm embrace:

'Haha. Araz, I remember you', she says. She looks down at the remaining bottles.

'Well, Araz, you know, I have been making it for the last 30 years', she laughs. 'I don't get too many complaints'.

'You make it yourself, at home?', he continued.

'Yes, it was my grandmother's recipe. I think you met her. Never changed a thing. It is very refreshing when it is so hot'.

'I need something cold before I get back in that car', he said. 'I am a taxi driver these days. I am going to Yalta now'. He buys two bottles.

'Yalta!', she said smiling. She clasped her hands firmly, 'oh, you know, I spent my childhood there. I would love to swim in the sea again'.

The olive-skinned man held out his hand. 'Why don't you join me? I would be pleased for the company. I like to talk to people when driving'.

'Really?' Her mind buzzed with the impromptu suggestion. The waves had been crashing in her mind all day, washing up childhood memories of freedom. And now this. 'But, but, I am not sure'...she said hesitantly. 'I still have to sell my last two bottles of *kvass*'.

Very discreetly, Araz places two rolled up hundred-ruble notes into her hand and closes it to show the negotiation is sealed. He quickly packs up the stall, places the two bottles under his arm and offers his free arm to her, escorting her to the car. He dashes around the car, opens the door for her and only closes it gently once she has ensured her dress is entirely clear of the door frame.

The journey takes them to the south, towards the mountains and to landscapes which for some may not appear Russian at all. Slurping intermittently on the *kvass*, Araz gives her a potted history of his life and talks himself into a state of excitement. She has heard it at least twice before, and so remains silent. He speaks and speaks but she only retains the words she was expecting. Araz was originally from Azerbaijan. He had moved to Crimea twenty-five years ago for love (a love which had *not* worked out) and made it his home:

'Nobody knows Crimea as well as me', he declared proudly. There was a breathlessness at the end of his sentences.

Heavy rain begins to fall, sluicing the windows of the car. The raindrops are as thick as almonds. They pass villages with Turkish names, castles, palaces and fortresses built in a curious *mélange* of architectural styles but faithful to none. With their *corps de logis* comprising a confusing medley of Islamic and English Tudor Renaissance styles, these eccentric summer residences served the Russian royal family, Nazi opportunists and obscure aristocrats:

'All kinds of nations and polities have had their hands on Crimea' offers Araz as if she were a tourist.

Araz's lively speech was no doubt inspired by vanity, to make her set aside the miserable state in which he had found her.

As they approach the coast, the air begins to smell of juniper. There is a hard beauty to the Crimean Mountains that shelter the bay of Yalta. Not so long ago, wolves roamed here; sufferers of tuberculosis were treated in its sanatoriums. Now, well-fed traffic policemen and their roadblocks are the guardians of these windy lanes. Variegated, oleander-lined roads lead from the steep slopes down to the town spilling out into busy squares centered on statues of Chekhov and Lenin. Soon, once they have passed the pomegranate trees, she is able to hear the waves pile up. The roads are narrow and without pavements. Hemmed in, pedestrians hop into blossoming lilac shrubs as locals tear around the corners. This part of Crimea feels Sicilian with its vineyards, narratives of banditry and daring passings on blind curves. As in Sicily, it is said relationships are built here on courage, sacrifice and honor. Araz approved of all three.

The rain has stopped. She fixes her kindling eyes on the sea horizon in the distance and sighs deeply. 'Here lies my soul', she whispers to herself. Araz drives her down to the embankment:

'I return to Simferopol tonight. I can take you back. No problem. Enjoy your freedom', he smiles.

She glances briefly at Araz and places her right hand on her thumping heart. No longer locked in the car, she skips to the embankment railing, spreads her arms out on the smooth metal and breathes in the fresh sea air. The wind ruffles her clothes, her hair. Last time she was here it was Easter, after the news of a death, and women were queuing outside churches to have their *kulich* blessed. Now, the tangy iodine scent of the churning sea lifted instantly her feelings and reminded her of those childhood days when she and her sister dragged sun-weathered driftwood up the beach. The beaches were not gorged with people then. In a generous light, the sea at the shoreline is turquoise, then dark blue further out to sea but never black.

The surf is strong and makes a tremendous rasping sound as it drags the pebbles up and down the shoreline. She closes her eyes and smiles as she listens to this ceaseless rhythm, the lungs of life. She had missed the repeated refrain of the ebb and flow, the sense of loss and hope, the sea's moods. The indifferent, eternal repetitions cleared her mind, healed her fragile soul and attracted all those thinkers. The waves crashing on their destiny bring blurry images of the places they came from: Turkey, Romania, Bulgaria – mysterious, far-off lands hidden behind torn clouds.

Like exiles, Russians from the big cities have come to Yalta for the sea and the sun. Just like in the Soviet days. The beach is a confusion of humanity, strewn with bodies in the prone position and children marching inflatable paraphernalia towards the sea. They shout monosyllabic words to one another. On the stone breakwaters is written *kupat'sya zapreshcheno* 'swimming is prohibited'. The undertow is strong; small children struggle to race up the beach face as the froth explodes around their legs, but the temptation of the sea is too much for children and adults alike. The bathers arrive early in the morning and leave late in the afternoon. Free again, this is their life each year for a week or two.

She had hoped to find some dreamy quietude and grasp the beauty of the voices circulating in her memory. Her sister's that was now gone. She walks instead the promenade which like most seaside resorts seemed to her as one long class continuum: at one end was the Moscow set with their napkins, cocktails on the beach, background dance grooves and finger bowls and at the other people from 'the provinces' chewed on *semechki* ('sunflower seeds') – a habit that was considered uncouth in pre-revolutionary times –, Russian rap plays from Ladas with blacked out windows and diners handling Pizza wipe their greasy fingers on their shorts. She walks the whole length of the embankment, past endless hotel-touts, watching the late afternoon sun burn out over her shoulder. She thought of Chekhov as she passed young ladies with little white dogs on leads. She wanted the city to sink into darkness, so that she could have the beach to herself.

At that point she remembered a small alcove at the far end of the embankment beyond the railway station. She was certain that the armies of tourists would not know of this hidden place. Full of a sudden energy, she broke into a half-jog. Navigating the back streets – not wishing to be followed –, she soon came to the hole in the pavement where you could climb down onto a series of boulders and then onto the small strip of beach where she used to hide from her sister as a child. Heart pumping, she lowered herself down into the oubliette like entrance to the beach. The empty beach spawned schools of memories:

'It is like one of those lost paradises', she mumbled to herself.

Thrilled at rediscovering this sanctuary, she undressed, placed her cloudy-brown dress on the pebbles and floundered awkwardly over the stones towards the sea. Far from the sinister foam and scum, the water in this secluded bay was calm following the afternoon downpour and a pleasant temperature. She plunges into the sea, listening all the time to the waves lapping on the shore. The regularity of the waves sets her at peace. It was the end of the day. The street lights flick on with a faint buzz; their reflection shimmers on the softly undulating water. She swims breaststroke over the ripples, grinning at the regained freedom the sea has bestowed on her. The water slaps against her cheeks which spread to a smile. Seaweed tickles her ankles. She swims further out to sea until the laughter of small children on the embankment falls silent. She wants to be alone out here with just the soft sounds of splashing water – anchorless and free like an eternal sleep:

'Lyubov, Lyubov', shouts a distant voice from the grieving shadows on the beach.

'I thought you might be here. I told you nobody knows Crimea better than me', said Araz cheerily, an empty bottle of *kvass* in his hand.

A late summer afternoon in Crimea

Old Russia

Seeking the old pieties

FROM A FLOATING PLATFORM, a pianist played Borodin to the last remaining members of a wedding party. A few of us watched him from the poplar lined embankment; his hands darted up and down the keys with agreeable dexterity. It was a late Saturday evening in early July. The day had been hot; the light evening breeze refreshed the promenaders who were enjoying the last moments of the day. I sat, looking out across the still Volga – Europe's nomadic frontier – before the light faded completely.

I came to Yaroslavl on the slow train. It took four hours of hollow, rhythmic panting from Moscow. The sleeper train's vinyl covered benches make for a comfortable enough bed, but they were not designed for being sat on for hours on end. It had thus felt like a long journey. The train was full. Full with, I suspect, commuters returning to the suburbs and the countryside for the weekend. A few wore medical masks. Some wore them casually under the chin in the manner of an office worker who loosens his tie the moment he leaves the office. A train guard marched through the carriages holding what resembled a plastic water pistol. We all had our temperature taken: forehead and wrist. The guard read aloud the readings as if they were lottery tickets: 36.6, 37.0, 36.9. Her officious assistant jotted down the digits on a clip-board.

A pandemic had swept across Russia. After four months of being cooped up in a Moscow flat with all kinds of restrictions on my freedom, I sat glued to the window anxious to see something new. A greyness hung in the air. The two women sat opposite me live in one of Moscow's satellite towns and insist the view is bleak and that there is nothing to see – a land too harsh for picnics. At this stage of post self-isolation freedom, even a few jazzy billboards would spike an interest. I make light conversation with the women. There is the odd disconnected smile. Occasionally, a few hushed words would wrestle through their shyness. I listen to the subdued speech of Russia – the whispery sibilants and palatal fricatives buzzing around my ears, the lack of localness in their speech. One is an accountant; the other a trainee lawyer. The trainee lawyer is dark, slender and *soignée*. They offer monosyllabic answers to my questions peculiar for their ill-declined adjectives. There is a Chekhovian frustration in their sighs. They soon withdraw to their iPods and I fish around in my bag for my recently acquired Russian book on English pronunciation. I found it in a hipster book stall in a trendy part of Moscow where piles of books were being given away for free. The book was written in the 1950s and was full of strikingly dated phrases. Sometimes, the author had managed to mistranslate completely the Russian idiom. At least, the Russian must be correct I thought as I slipped it into my bag, and I might have some fun working out the correct English translations.

As the train crept through Moscow's commuter suburbs whose buildings with their multi-colored façades were covered with 'white lives matter' graffiti, I puzzled over when we might actually say 'to return to our muttons', 'the invalid is doing splendidly' or 'Vivie's vain of her voice'. Beyond the endless grids of late Brezhnev era housing projects, we pass through patches of forest, meadows of wild violet and weed-smeared ponds. Then, there were the Soviet garages – a sub-culture of hoarders where not yet entirely urbanized older men seem to store anything and everything in preparation for the next crisis. The value of material goods lingers in their minds. The accountant catches me scrutinizing the long rows of garages. She looks at me, says nothing and then looks at the garages whilst flicking her neck with her index and middle finger indicating that there are drunks there. These garages found all over Russia seem to belong in some kind of liminal space between town and countryside. The tatty garages and a promiscuity of children scrambling around the muddy lanes soon recede to the distance. The scenery becomes more rustic. Approaching Yaroslavl, there are freshly harvested fields that could almost be England.

It was early evening when I arrived in Yaroslavl. In that initial hour or so, the traveler's impressions are at their most acute. The world is all before you. The buzz of a new language humming around your ears can be magical. Your breathing changes as you hunt for meaning, quickly trying to create webs of familiarity to give you some sense of security. But, this was Yaroslavl, not Medellín or Accra. The streets were sleepy; the intoxication ephemeral. The odd cat appeared from the uncut grass surrounding one of the derelict churches. Preparing to roost, the starlings had gathered on the trolley bus cables that cobwebbed the sky. The railway station is situated far from the historic city center and my Azeri taxi driver curses as dented flotsam piles up on the busy streets. In between punches on the car horn, he waxes lyrical about politics and Azerbaijan's relationship with neighboring Armenia, 'very bad now, *voina, voina*! Soon, there will be war'. He raises his arms in a hieratic gesture. He aspirates his consonants and inserts all kinds of unstressed vowels: *priviet tovairishi*. His voluptuous words burst into the space of the afternoon. Even as I am about to leave the car, he continues to talk without pausing for breath as if my presence were of little relevance.

Far from the hustle and bustle, the old city exudes its bygone age charm on the Volga embankment which is lined with crumbling mansions in different shades of oranges and pinks. Their gardens are entered through wrought iron arches of a different era entirely. The embankment sweeps round the edges of the city and is dotted with white pavilions where couples pause to have their photograph taken. After the gloom of the Khrushchyovka with their coin operated lifts which fill the suburbs of most Russian cities (Yaroslavl included), this tableau of faded elegance takes you back to another world, what this country had been. The splendor of imperial Russia.

Walking the embankment, it is not difficult to imagine how a hundred years ago this stretch of the Volga would have appeared. *Volga-Matushka* ('Mother Volga'): Europe's largest and longest river drains most of western Russia. This national artery twists and turns its way for over 2,000 miles until it reaches the Caspian Sea. As the empire came to an end, this section of the river would have been packed with paddle steamers. Aboard, Tsarist gentlemen believed this life could continue forever as they promenaded up and down the decks discussing their annals of love, doffing their hats to passing ladies. Plenitudes were borne. Captains in splendid uniforms pulled on cords and the steamer's whistles echoed down the embankment where excited crowds waved to their departing relatives. These nostalgic sounds fill my mind as I trace the footsteps of the porters who carried the wares of passengers headed for hotels and nearby mansions.

With these images and sounds swirling in my thoughts, I spent the first day traversing parks organized around impressive statues ranging from Lenin in various poses to Nekrasov to brown bears on my way to one splendid seventeenth century church or another. Yaroslavl's skyline is bustling with golden, green and blue cupolas that reach up to the heavens like expectant rose buds. The post-virus streets were still quiet, the museums locked, the restaurants half-empty. Each evening as the day drew to a close, screaming parties of swifts began to dart in and out of the belfries. The commotion would last until the sun dipped below the horizon, and then the streets would become quiet again.

Wondering whether I had seen what I needed to see in Yaroslavl, I asked the head-scarfed lady selling candles at the Kirillo-Afanasiyevskiy Monastery what she liked most about the city. She leant towards me and whispered 'the three onions. You have seen?' I thought perhaps she was referring to one of the many churches or monasteries, but no 'the three onions' is a sculpture of the Holy Trinity. 'If you like, I show you'. She quickly closed the shop door, crossed herself and under turquoise domes marched me across the city pass gardens brimming with hollyhocks. Elena had lived her whole life in Yaroslavl, preferring the slower pace of life here compared to Moscow. She had studied theology and it was her interest in icons which led her to work in the monastery:

'The icon, yes, that is the outward sign of the inward grace', she continued trying to catch her breath.

The sculpture she is referring to was inspired by the Trinity Icon by Andrey Rublev.

'Rublev was great Russian painter in fifteenth century, you know. He brought harmony to country. There was plague and Tatar invaders. A difficult time, I think'.

She speaks in a fever of rushed syllables:

'Slavery. Yes. Russia is history of slavery, you know?', she says in an afterthought.

'Icon, I mention of three angels became most famous of all Russian icons. Original in Tretyakov Gallery in Moscow. You have probably seen. You will forgive me. I need to get back to shop. Enjoy your stay'.

Elena was gone in a flash, a spry, black headscarf zig-zagging between promenaders. The sculpture seemed much less impressive to me than the magnificent cathedral that glistened in the afternoon sunshine behind it.

The pandemic had kept most visitors away. In local restaurants, I was treated like a special guest – a pioneer amongst stay-at-homes who had braved everything to get his *pelmeni* and sour cream. Under the gaze of curious tabbies, I walked from church to church, past ancient theatres and sorrowful World War II memorials that are to be found in every Russian city. In the churches there were just one or two souls – typically old women bent over in the shape of question marks whispering supplications and seeking the mystery of revelation. Down the road, *zhigulis* whizzed past the old pieties – Lenin sits on his stool looking out over the new part of the city pontificating on the struggle between the material and the ideal.

After three days in Yaroslavl, I head back to tar scented Moscow in order to take the train to Vladimir and then travel by taxi to Suzdal. I travel *platzkart*. This is the third class, doorless sleeper carriage (part train, part dormitory), and for many still a part of Russian life. Here, people from all across the country quickly meld together, sharing stories and food. Despite the pandemic, there are bodies strewn everywhere. It is early morning. The few Russians that have joined the train at Yaroslavl quickly swap their shoes for slippers, anxious not to introduce any dirt into the train carriage. Many of the passengers are beginning to stir as the *provodnitsa* walks the corridor offering breakfast tea. In search of my place, I weave in and out of smelly feet protruding from bunks and hop over the remains of Pot Noodles, *vatrushka* and cabbage *pirogi*. Some of the snoring army cadets look like they have more or less moved in. I find what I believe is my bunk, but am soon redirected by a fat, bare-torsoed man whose place I have just taken. Patting his impressive bulk, he spends the entire journey eating – *kholodets*, *blini* and pepper sprinkled *salo*. I have a top bunk and am pressed close to the ceiling. As the train is packed with passengers sleeping, I have little choice but lie down and relax for the duration of the relatively short journey to Moscow. It is one of the occasions where if you have found your place, you don't leave it.

Once in Moscow, I negotiate the fury of the 'garden' ring road to yet another railway station (*Kazanskiy vokzal*) and take the train to Vladimir. This time, I travel in the second class *kupe*. I share a compartment with three engineers who are headed to Perm in the Urals. They are louche looking men with sweaty brows. I try to unpack the hidden images behind their words. They speak of forlorn hopes. I observe their very refined and well-rehearsed train etiquette. In the train compartment, they switch to a familiar military like routine, changing into their 'train clothes' and slippers, laying out their food on the communal fold-down table and packing everything else away in the compartment under the seat. This is clearly a well-rehearsed exercise and home for the next day or so. Anxious to give them a bit of space, I walk the corridors in search of an elusive socket to charge my mobile phone. When I rejoin them, I am invited to abjure my native victuals and chew on dried fish. My foreign gaze seems particularly conspicuous this afternoon. The men want to know if it is difficult to find work in my country and what the hourly pay might be for an engineer. I fumble around for some answers and am reminded of the strangeness in the ordinary.

I arrive in Vladimir under a blistering heat. I soon find a taxi to take me to Suzdal. My driver is a young man from Donetsk. 'What are you doing here, if it is not a secret?', he asks. We soon get chatting about languages. He asks me how the Slavic languages are related, what is the oldest language in the world, what do I think of the Hebrew language and what is the relationship between spoken and written Sanskrit. As we approach Suzdal, we pass freshly harvested fields with white-washed, onion-domed churches dotting the river that snakes through the village. There are churches and chapels everywhere, straddling the river, lying in fields of hay, on every street corner. Wooden, stone, red, white, yellow and most striking of all, multi-colored. From the car window, a lyrical landscape of medieval symbols spreads out like a Savrasov painting absorbing all the nineteenth century rural idyll motifs. With its wooden gingerbread like houses and chimney smoke drifting over the still river, Suzdal is every bit a fairy tale location. Moscow with its conglomeration of humanity and its hinterland of Soviet tower blocks seems centuries away, hiding in another world almost.

It was just before 5pm when I made it to Suzdal on one of those summer afternoons where everything seemed perfect. The sky was cloudless; the women's summer dresses were white and unblemished, the churches' spires sparkled in the sunshine. A heavenly tranquility had descended on the place. The occasional tractor chugs down the lane to a background of gentle clip-clopping of horse's hooves in the distance. I had come to the old country.

The evening services were about to begin in the thirty-seven churches, chapels and monasteries that make up this ancient village of 10,000 people. A campanological flair pealed out across the town reminding us the Orthodox liturgical day was about to begin. All these churches date to the late seventeenth and early eighteenth centuries. One by one, the bells stopped, the orchestra wound down and the village became seductively still. I walk from church to church, spying through ancient keyholes looking for the yoke of wisdom. Priests dressed in raven black and wearing fancy headdresses known as *kamilavka* chant in Church Slavonic to two or three ecclesiastically distanced elderly women who scrutinize my movements as I tentatively join them in the spiritual sensorium of mimetic gesture. These matriarchs – the guardians of Russian propriety – look me over with misgiving.

I enter a different world entirely – a synesthetic mingling of spiritual and physical senses –, and am soon enveloped in clouds of incense and foreign consonants. The priest speaks of transgressions, the miserable state of mankind and how we are all defeated by corruptibility. The *babushkas* bow and cross themselves repeatedly; the fire of contrition burns brightly and their faith flourishes in their hearts. But this is a land of mourners and we are all trying to draw closer to God, trying to disentangle the ineffable mysteries of the soul. I imagine the same scenes unfolding in each chapel and monastery in Suzdal. These elderly widows have lived through the Soviet period, *perestroika* and now find themselves the cultural anchor of New Russia. The next hour is full of the sounds of chinking censors and mystical chants that navigate the link between the verbal and the sensing. Rapid readings from the Scriptures cast us back centuries and more as our perceptual powers try to juggle the divine-human alignment. This hour belongs to my memories, and after attending many such services I begin to wonder if I still need the Protestant aisles.

Vespers complete, we are dismissed with the usual benediction. Prepared for the sleep of the night and the dawn of the new day to come, I take my leave. The priest prays in private and the *babushkas* busy themselves with tasks to close the church for the day.

I walk the shaded lanes, past smoked mackerel vendors and head towards the river where couples photograph themselves in front of a sun melting in different hues of bronze. Soon, the priest who just presided over our service saunters past. He drags his angular shadow of solemnity behind him:

'Good evening, Father, thank you for the service', I offer.

His dusky eyes settle on me: the dregs of sorrow on a late summer's afternoon. With his long flowing chestnut beard and black cassock, this tall figure makes for a haunting presence. He asks me if I am just visiting Suzdal and whether I have been here before.

'Come I will show you the burial mounds', he says.

Adjacent to apple green meadows lie the people who built Suzdal's ramparts and cathedral in the twelfth century.

'This would have been the cemetery' he says, pointing to a few hillocks.

'The early people of Suzdal are buried here. The unpaid serfs, I imagine'.

Oblivious to the previous hardships, young children race up the mounds, and play King of the Hill at the top. Their laughter rings out across the village; their humor constructs an unreal world impervious to adults. For centuries, Suzdal was the scene of a cocktail of uprisings, invasions and bloody battles. Poles, Mongols and Crimean Tatars had all invaded and left their mark. There was the plague, conflagrations and endless disputes between Princes. And now in the twenty-first century, there was a pandemic:

'But somehow Suzdal survived it all and went on to become an important religious center', he continues.

We walk under the silhouettes of wooden churches that prod the sky. His speech is gracious and seasoned with salt:

'By the sixteenth century, no other town in Russia had as many churches as Suzdal. But, not all religious', he laughs. 'Weddings took place at night. It is said the clergy danced until dawn', he grins. He offers his hand. 'Sergei. Pleased to meet you'.

With his index finger he paints a long, horizontal arc in the air until it rests on a complex of white washed buildings in the distance. 'You will miss all this when you go back to Moscow. I am headed in that direction', he says. 'God be with you', and he heads off up the lane towards the monastery.

I find a nearby restaurant and dine on *vareniki* watching the bleeding sun crash below the horizon and pondering the grammar of the Orthodox life. Two days later, I am on the train back to Moscow and have occasion to hear the priest's voice. His words circulate in my mind: God *is* love and Christ is the image of the beauty of God. Russians have always seen the search for beauty and truth as linked to the worship of God.

The train is by far the most modern I have been on in Russia– no *platzkart, provodnitsa* offering tea or engineers from the Urals in their pajamas. I cannot find anything Russian about it and for a moment feel as if I could be anywhere. But then, we pass through commuter towns with ungraspable names. The train stops briefly at one called Zheleznodorozhny. The lady opposite taps my knee: 'You know Tolstoy and Anna Karenina?' 'Yes, well, the main character committed suicide here'.

Somewhere in Siberia
Meeting the high priest of the banya

MY FIRST SIGHTING OF Siberia was the vast taiga that stretched out beneath me. The sun was already up. The forest seemed boundless. There was no sign of human civilization: no roads, buildings, houses, cars. Just forest that gave way eventually to what appeared to be flat scrubland and in the far distance the occasional oil refinery. The scrubland was in fact a swamp the size of France.

Siberia is a land of imponderable extremes. An area larger than Europe and the US combined, here, in the winter, the temperature falls to minus 40 degrees. This summer, new records have been set as the mercury flirted with plus 40 degrees. Soon, I spotted the vein of the Tom – calm and sparkling in the morning sunshine – meandering its way through the vacant land towards the city. As we approached Tomsk, splashes of color flashed beneath me from the wooden houses that made up scruffy villages clustered by the river.

Not wishing to risk three days cooped up in a train in the middle of the worst pandemic for a century, I had taken the red-eye from Moscow. Black kites scattered as we skid on the runway. Apart from the lone semaphorist, the landing strip was empty. Sat in front of me were two stern-looking men with ear pieces. Uniformed and without face masks or boarding cards, they walked a very heavy hold all off the plane. On the tarmac, two armed men stood by a waiting van. The men hopped into the van and disappeared quickly from sight, leaving my co-passengers whispering and gossiping. The smell of burning rubber from our dramatic landing lingered in the air.

This seemed like the last place to witness any kind of drama. When I arrived, the city was still sleeping. My driver, Sergei, was waiting for me diligently at Arrivals. He pinched his nose:

'Good morning. Phew...I am sorry. The smell of rubber. Your first time in Tomsk? You will like. It is quiet, calm city. No rushing around like in Moscow'. He produces words in a vivid, straightforward melody.

His voice soon adopts a narrative tone. Proud of his city, Sergei proceeded to run through Tomsk's achievements: city founded in 1604, Tomsk State University founded in 1880, the first Russian city to have the Internet etc. He is steeped in the exceptional achievements of his city and when he speaks about them his voice is stifled with urgency. He draws out and softens his sentences.

The journey from the airport takes us through the forest. Russian Orthodox icons of Saint Nicholas the Wonderworker hang from his rearview mirror – visions of sugar plums dance in my head. The sunlight glides through patches of ghostly silver birch. 'Look, Russian trees', Sergei smiles. His smile is thin; his eyes rueful. He likes to edit my Russian, reorganizing my faulty stress placement. Many Russians remain convinced the birch can only be found in Russia. Sergei points to a new housing development on the left comprising palatial detached houses: *Tam bagatiye* 'there live the rich', he says. He nods knowingly, 'money from oil', I think. The city benefited from the spike in oil prices ten years ago. The Trans-Siberian Railway bypasses Tomsk and the city was consigned to relative economic isolation for the best part of a century. Record high oil prices changed all of that, but now the boom is over the city's ambitions have again been tamed, its inhabitants humbled perhaps.

We soon arrived at my late nineteenth century hotel which was full of promise and charm on the outside, but rather lacking either on the inside. I was the only guest and my arrival had coincided with the Russian annual shutdown of hot water. My breakfast came each morning in a plastic bag and with a fully stretched out arm, was dangled in front of me. I was told to eat it in my room. 'The virus, new regulations', a lean young man told me with an expression as somber as a departing night. Any prestige that a foreigner might have had in the Soviet period was long gone. It was a pandemic and we all had to play by the rules. The hotel was in fact run by this pale teenager who sat on an old Chesterfield in the entrance hallway glued to the television, quickly stubbing out Sobranie cigarettes as I entered. We shared parts of my language, and then parts of his. Neither party sought to seize control of the conversation. He paused occasionally to crush a mosquito against the wall. He told me in no uncertain terms that the pandemic had devastated their business. *Plokha, ochen plokha*, he would say with the corners of his mouth turned down.

Tomsk is laid out around two main streets running parallel to one another, north to south. The side streets (such as Soviet Street) that run between these two axes are filled with late nineteenth century wooden houses. Most of them are in need of urgent repair, but the intricate wood-carved window frames and lace roof architecture typical of Siberia are still intact. Not far from the city center, beyond the blueberry street vendors, there is a wooden church resembling a multi-tiered Norwegian stave church. Soviet Street was one of my favorite streets. The city is full of trams, and here a tramway runs right up the middle of this narrow lane. The street is overgrown with poplars and weeds. It was as if the city residents had simply forgotten about it. The subsiding fairytale like mansions stand at sixty-degree angles, leaning into their pre-Soviet heritage. Cats, the proprietors of this rewilded street, stalk the pathways observing the essence of all things.

Jet-lagged, I stumble through the streets, somewhat startled by the talking traffic lights. Sweat begins to leak from my brow. It is still morning and already thirty degrees. Kites hang over the city. The heat wave and pandemic had left the streets more or less empty. I was one of the very few tourists in Tomsk this virus-ridden summer. Despite the circumstances, square shaped Soviet buses ply constantly the Prospekt Lenina with its impressive art nouveau buildings. The distinctive sound of these buses' engines and slow, purposeful gear changes take my mind back to Colombia and West Africa: Cali and Ouagadougou – cities defined by noise, dance and color. Prospekt Lenina is on a slight incline and feeds into the impressive Novosobornaya Square, a carrefour of Soviet butcheries. Just as I pause to read about the history of the square, I get the attention of a passerby who is at first reluctant to speak to me but then offers:

'The cathedral was blown up here in 1934. They replaced it with statues of Lenin. God was dead, officially', he grins. 'All replaced by ideology', he continues. 'In Russia, all we fear is change. People assume change will only result in things getting worse'.

Before I can ask him my short-list of questions, he is gone, breaks into a light jog and hops onto the *paziki* to join those preoccupied with the cares of everyday existence. On the bus, he semi-bows and stands holding his hand to his heart as a gesture of asking forgiveness. The precursor of humility is meekness.

I criss-cross the rose-scented square that fills handsomely the center of the city. Heavy trams grind and rumble around its circumference. Sat on a park bench, a man – expelled from life – with a purple, weathered face grabs pigeons, decapitates them with a quick twist of the wrist and places their writhing bodies into a plastic bag. Otherwise, the square is empty. In the hot summer evenings, the Tomich (as the residents are known) walk in the recently refashioned park that nowadays makes up the square. The street loudspeakers that line Prospekt Lenina and the roads surrounding the park no longer broadcast propaganda, but remind the city-dwellers of Covid 19 etiquette: stay at least 1.5 meters away from the nearest person, wear face masks in shops and use hand-wash. During the Soviet period when the churches were locked up, the day started not with the ringing of bells but with the national anthem blaring from these same loudspeakers. And then it would be played once again to mark the end of the day. It started as a moment of ideological salience but faded into everyday trivia. Habit is everything.

Further up the hill from Novosobornaya Square lie a collection of impressive classical buildings that house half a dozen universities of some repute. Here, Tomsk feels European, not remotely like a city in the fastness of western Siberia. Tomsk is a student city, but the virus has rendered the lecture theatres empty. Those looking to exchange intelligent views on Heidegger and Heine had been exiled to I don't know where. There is just the odd begowned student who has graduated in much reduced in size graduation ceremonies. As well as the universities, the restaurants and cafés were all closed. I wandered in and out of hotels looking for a cup of coffee, but was greeted with shrugged shoulders and a barrage of one-word negatives that draw any hope of a conversation to an immediate close: *nyet* ('no'), *nelzya* ('must not'), *nichevo* ('nothing'). It seemed I had come a week too early. Everything was to open up following the week.

There were just a few exceptions: the churches, a second-hand bookshop and *banya* whose appeal was somewhat lessened by the current heat wave. The bookshop was delightful for its lack of modern accoutrements – no big 'pay here' signs suspended from the ceiling or indeed tills of any kind, just a bohemian woman with tangled hair who tucked the cash into her back pocket. After a few jovial misunderstandings with the plump bookshop proprietor, her husband I imagine, I left laden down with LPs of

Russian male choirs and retreated into some Russian spirituality. A country as endless as this makes you in the end start looking for your inner freedom. Always seeking the transcendental, I tracked down the impressive churches that offer an insight into Siberia's tumultuous past. As well as the Orthodox churches, there is a Catholic and Lutheran church, the latter in its original guise would have been used by seventeenth century Swedish prisoners of war. In the Stalin era, it was turned into a berry juice factory before being demolished and only rebuilt in 2006. Another church served as a temporary prison during the Purge of 1937-38 for dissidents before they were sent to the camps.

Down the road, I push open the heavy door to the Orthodox cathedral – this spiritual hospital for those besieged by sin, seeking salvation or an incorruptible grace. I, the wayward traveler exiled in shackles, enter the hallowed, indispensable silence. My thoughts turn to the local Saint, Saint Domna. She had been exiled to Tomsk after having been arrested on a holy pilgrimage. Her relatives intended to force her into marriage, but she wanted to preserve her virginity for the Lord's sake. She left behind a wealthy background and chose to live in abject poverty with a multitude of stray dogs. Through her divine homage and having taken upon herself the yoke of Christ, she joined the ranks of the pure for she did not malign the word of God.

A few people stand in the ante-chapel. Confessants queue, asking to have their transgressions wiped away whereas I, the rebellious intellect imperiled by doubt, come here so that the senses can re-instruct the mind. Dripping candle wax and whispers: God is listening to the accounts of the mortals. The penitents swap their future shame for their present shame. The original grace lost, they can only offer up supplicatory words as collateral but God knows they are not intrinsically bad. God is love; love is kind; God is kind: the chain of syllogisms goes on and on. And the confessants' words can change everything for they might result in spiritual renewal. Tomorrow, they will sup from the sacramental spoon and a new chapter of salvation will begin. United in the indissoluble bond of love.

* * *

It was not long before I found the public *banya*. This one is Soviet in style and would have been used as frequently as perhaps three times a week by Tomich in the Soviet period. During those years, many Russians lived in communal flats (*kommunalkas*) and bathroom facilities were shared with strict timetables. To escape all the restrictions, many just came to the *banya* instead.

The *banya* remains an important part of Russian culture. Unlike in some Finnish saunas, the *banya* for men and women are separate. Indeed, many *banya* used to alternate between men and women days. Russians go to the *banya* in groups and will typically spend several hours there, chit-chatting in their felt hats to protect their heads from the extreme heat. The ritual begins with a shower before entering the *parilka* or steam room. Russians follow a strict cycle, rotating between the *banya* where the temperature might be 100 degrees Celsius and several dips in a wooden bath of cold water:

'Head must go *under* water three times', says sternly the *banyachik*, the high priest of the *banya* who is here to show me the dos and don'ts as I exit the *parilka*.

If the cold water bath has little appeal, you can opt to pull the rope outside the steam room and a wooden bucket full of ice cold water will up-end and come crashing down on your head. Unable to resist the challenge, Vladimir, the *banyachik*, grins as I pull the rope. There is an audible gasp for breath as the shock of cold water explodes over my head. 'Very good, very good', he says encouragingly. His face is round and jovial; full of pledges of kindness, I suspect. He has wide blue eyes and the neck of a wrestler. Occasionally, he would square his shoulders.

Laid out on the top wooden bench of the bathhouse where it is hottest, Vladimir then beats me with hot dried branches of pine called *venik*. These have been soaking in hot water for twenty minutes beforehand to make them soft. Vladimir places also branches of hot pine on my head. The scent of the forest is overwhelming. Whilst telling me about how pine improves blood circulation, Vlad flutters the *venik* above my back creating an airflow that warms up still further the body. He talks about *banya* as if it were an abstract philosophy; he speaks in complex analogies. Then follows a routine of stroking, flailing and beating with the branches and finally a kind of compression where the leaves are pushed into the body for a few seconds. It is not painful, but the heat of the pine is at times difficult to bear.

The *venik* flagellation complete, Vladimir and I sit on the lower bench and bury our heads in the pine branch breathing in slowly and deeply. His plump face wears earnest lines. When he speaks of *banya* etiquette, his words take on an absolute seriousness. The pine needles are hot, almost too hot to hold to your face. This whole routine is repeated three times. After a shower, we then sit in the adjacent room, snack on salt-dried Caspian roach (*vobla*) and drink ice cold vodka. The feeling after *banya* is one of incomparable relaxation. You feel sleepy, content and completely at ease. The heaviness of the world is gone. 'Sleep after *banya*, deep and long', Vlad says as if he is reading my thoughts.

A glint in his eye, Vladimir raises his glass to me, 'my friend, you did well', *s' lyogkim parom* – which I am told is a traditional toast made after *banya* that means 'have a light steam'.

'Light steam. To be frank, I feel a little light-headed', I tell him. The shocks from the extreme heat and cold ricochet around my body producing some kind of vaguely pleasant tingling sensation.

'Come, let us go outside now', instructs Vlad. We go outside into the fury of the sunlight. In the perpetually grey days of a Russian winter, going outside is normally the last spasmodic shock to the system, but today's heat is dry and penetrating.

Late afternoon, somewhere in Siberia (my head is spinning), we stand in our dressing gowns and flip-flops on a street lined with dreary Soviet housing blocks. Traffic dives past us. I am subliminally aware of, what is to a foreigner at least, the strangeness of the situation. I almost forget what I am doing here. The geometry of the streets quivers for a moment; the brutal architecture, an ideological curse, wobbles. Clad in bathrobes, small groups of men chat, smoke cigarettes and drink ice cold beer whilst sweat pours from their steamed brows. Their clouds of cigarette smoke become silky in the sunlight. Vlad entertains them with his jokes about the 'willing foreigner', packing more and more words into single breaths. Reunited with native speakers, he begins to heap up masses of words rendering them into an idiomatic Russian that is just out of my reach. The flow of words speeds up. He uses short, crude phrases and speaks in whispering syllables. He likes to latch onto people, and tease them before looking around to see if his listeners are tired of his badinage.

On their way home from work and with leather satchels under arm, commuters of sorts in ill-fitted suits and elastic gaits hop off the *paziki* that stop like clockwork every few minutes on the street. Their shadows chase them down the *trottoir*.

'You do sport?', Vlad asks me with a smile of expectation and a phlegmatic voice. Every part of the *banya* experience is ritualized, and the conversation between men immediately after *banya* is no exception. This is a chance to probe your fellow bather's masculinity. Vladimir is a retired swimming instructor. He flexes his arms as if to show me his classic musculature. 'I have spent my life surrounded by water', he jokes as he chews on *shashlik*. Puffed up with knowledge, questions stampede out as his mental vigor overflows. Did I like Sherlock Holmes? Did I miss home? Was I from London?, he would ask repeatedly with the back of his tongue touching his throat in that distinctive Russian way of pronouncing the 'L'. What did I think of Margaret Thatcher? And most memorably, 'Did I feel my genus?'. After each collection of thoughts, he would bring his sentences to an end with a long drawn out *vot* 'there you have it'. Vlad speaks affectionately of his family and the charms of kinship. The conversation was far removed from the *banyachik* I met in Rublyovka (Moscow), a retired KGB General who lectured me on the very Russian art of picking wild mushrooms whilst thrashing me naked with birch.

The afternoon has become evening. I stifle a yawn. No longer feeling topsy-turvy, I take to my feet. A black cat runs past in front of us. Vlad's eyes liven:

'Oh, my friend. That is bad omen. Let's hope virus doesn't get us', he jokes.

A wave of tiredness hits me. Vlad takes my hand and squeezes it firmly 'sleep well, *tovarish* ('comrade'), I need to go to village'. He points towards the river. There was a Tomsk down there too, amongst the weeds and sun-worshipping *divorcées*. I return to my quiet, almost ghostly hotel adjacent to the sharp bend in the tram track. I had barely undressed when a heavy sleep descended on me. Memories intermingled with a debris of ideas float into the past. I had hoped to hear Russian in my dreams.

The main thoroughfare in Tomsk

The 13:24 to Gorky
Propaganda for sainthood

I ARRIVE AT THE station early. This is my first trip on a train with a dog in Russia. The information online regarding the dos and don'ts of pet travel in Russia had been somewhat conflicting and I am eager to be prepared for every potential bureaucratic niggle. I listen to the announcements on the public address system. What were last year a series of soft, buzzing sounds colliding with one another have become (partially at least) intelligible words. As the snow started to melt, the strange sounds turned into meaning. The appeal of this land started with these whispered, mellifluous sounds amidst icons, censers and pale-eyed belles dressed in furs.

Not so long ago, such a railway platform would have been choking with steam. There would have been the noise of heavy train doors slamming in quick succession just before the moment of departure, guards' whistles, mothers shouting teary farewells to their sons leaning out of the carriage windows. Now, the platform is near-empty. The passengers sit in the heated waiting room, browsing their iPhones, looking occasionally at the silent digital Passenger Information System which constantly alternates between Russian, Chinese and English.

Trying to keep warm and preferring generally to be outside, I walk briskly up and down the Kursky railway station platform. I am armed with pet passports, vaccination certificates, veterinarian letters translated into Russian and copies of pet transport regulations, but it is thankfully all in vain. A thorough check of the documents by the *provodnitsa* and I am allowed on the train and shown to my half-compartment. I am on my way to Nizhny Novgorod. The 13:24. Nizhny is a four-hour train ride east of Moscow that takes you through Vladimir – an ancient city of white

46

churches – and flashes of small villages. We pass Shishkinesque landscapes whose imagery is reminiscent of Russian epic literature. Our first-class compartment is bit of a treat for me and Stan, my two-year old spaniel. We have two comfortable leather seats, a fold down bed, a drop-leaf table and a tiny ensuite bathroom. It is going to be a far-cry from the third-class communal wagons (*platzkart*) where you might find card-playing, vodka drinking army cadets traveling for six days on the train from Vladivostok to Chechnya.

Moscow (indeed Russia) is a country designed with train travel in mind. There are eight *vokzal* (railway stations) dotted around the circumference of this impressive, bulging city, enabling you to reach the distant corners of Russia with minimal need for changes. Buying the ticket was quite a test of my Russian. Russian is famous for its panoply of verbs of motion, all of which combine with a dozen or so prefixes and have an imperfective and perfective form. As I experimented with various verbal permutations until my rather simple request was understood, the queue behind me at the counter in the Kursky railway station began to snake out of sight. The woman serving me had not sold a first-class ticket to somebody traveling with their dog before. Let alone a foreigner who spoke garbled Russian, putting the stress on the wrong syllable in every other word. At one point, six sets of pale blue eyes stared at the screen, debating I am not sure what. Behind me, brows began to furrow, arms waved in protest. *Sabiraetsya li on na Kamchatky?* 'Is he going to Kamchatka?', I heard one of them grumble.

Aboard the train, my *provodnitsa* introduces the compartment fittings and more importantly furnishes me with the menu for the adjacent dining car. As I have bought the compartment and not just a seat (one of the requirements when traveling with a pet on this particular train), I will be served two sets of everything. What is more, Stan is invited to join me. This is not the slow train and soon we speed pass endless lines of soulless, identical housing blocks splashed across the utilitarian canvas that is the Balashikha *oblast*. This dehumanizing Lego – architecture for a classless society – stretches through the edgelands of post-Soviet Russia. The socialist utopia of Moscow's satellite cities eventually fades into fields of thinly covered white snow and half-empty villages of wooden dachas. There is the occasional sun-dappled hillside. These two Russias – city and countryside – seem to be worlds apart.

I listen to the sound of footsteps in the corridor that runs alongside the compartments. Muffled voices speak laconic words. I hear the faint sound of coffee cups cluttering in their saucers. A knock at the door and the *provodnitsa* invites me to take lunch in the restaurant wagon. Toy penguin in mouth (the hippopotamus, beaver and elephant long since been destuffed), Stan joins me at the table. Refusing to let go of the fluffy toy, his eyes fix on the woody hunting grounds and the scummed ponds that soon disappear from sight. I contemplate my fellow passengers who speak in determined, harsh tones. An older gentleman sits taciturn, lost in thought as we train-travelers sometimes are when the outside world receding from us at such haste becomes blurred. The present merges into the future as fugitive tracks flee from sight. At the neighboring tables, bored couples who reckon their age in winters talk of how they could not remember such a mild February. Anton, my sturdy waiter, explains to me that I can have two of everything, but they have to be the same dish. *Seledka pod shuboy* (literally 'herring under the fur coat', small pieces of herring mixed with boiled potato, beetroot, carrot and mayonnaise) is brought to me with a beer and a bread-roll. And before I have a chance to consider the main course, another *seledka pod shuboy*, beer and bread-roll appears. After two additional Siberian *pelmeni* washed down with two cups of black tea with two bits of lemon, I am sufficiently replete all I want to do is retreat to my carriage for a post-prandial siesta.

We arrive in Nizhny in early evening under a psychedelic sunset. The railway station seems to lie in the margins of the city, partially hidden under its forgotten shadows. Nizhny, one of the former 'closed cities' of the Soviet Union, is carved into two by the immense Volga which at points is forty miles wide. Most of the sights are to be found on the east bank where the kremlin is situated. Up on the hill, the kremlin is a showcase of Soviet tanks, Eastern Front military paraphernalia, a cathedral, an impressive art museum and an architectural monstrosity whose function I forget. As with most kremlins, it is a kind of city within a city. 'Here they gunned down the Luftwaffe', a passing tour guide says with a proud grin. 'Nizhny provided the military equipment for the Front. Big factories here', he continues. The Germans bombed them for two years. Then, the city was known as Gorky after the writer Maxim Gorky who was something of a poster boy for the socialists. Every year he would be shortlisted for the Nobel Prize for Literature, just to be sent back to the city named after him and discover it had gone to Bunin.

Just beneath the kremlin lie the Chkalov Stairs, a monumental sweeping staircase with over five hundred steps. The staircase is named after the aviation pioneer, Chkalov who was the first person to fly a plane over the North Pole, and was built to outdo the famous Potemkin Stairs in Odessa. It is here where Stan and I take our morning constitutional, jogging from bottom to top with Stan always surging just ahead. We enjoy a well earnt rest at the top on a bench and take in the view which stretches out across the Volga, over the tops of Orthodox cathedrals in various shades of pink and persimmon into industrial gloom. Beyond, lies the town of Bor connected uniquely with Nizhny by cable car. On the neighboring bench, an elderly lady dressed in furs sits upright, scrutinizing something or other on the river:

'Is there anything to see in Bor?', I ask her. She turns, surprised at the question:

'No, ugly city. No need to visit'. As always, the Russians are brutally frank about what is worth seeing and what is not worth seeing in their country.

The sky is grey; the wind biting. There are rumors of more snow. Wishing to escape the cold and in search of Orthodox salvation, I go from church to church hopping on and off trams that grind down cobbled streets and sweep around the busy lanes. Stan's face glued to the window, we pass a collage of dissonance: neo-classical buildings, wooden houses and Soviet splurge. Viking traders once walked these streets. The churches' golden cupolas sit like rose buds behind ashen façades of Brezhnev apartment blocks. These housing blocks seem to serve as concrete curtains to hide Ceaușescu style the churches. Right at the end of the main street on the east bank lies the thirteenth century Annunciation Monastery where black-scarved nuns, bibles under arm, dart past me on electric scooters, weaving their way through the complex of white stone churches.

One afternoon, I ascend the steep hill to the upper tier of the city on the level of the kremlin. Here, off the main shopping thoroughfare lies the rather eccentric Russian Museum of Photography where at the entrance I am told 'the Museum will not be of interest if you are not interested in photography'. I confirm my interest in photography and persuade her to allow me to enter. I leave my coat at the *garderob* and spend an hour or so admiring Soviet rangefinder cameras piled up in dusty cabinets. Later in the day, I relax in busy cafés where poets once sat secluded from the gnawing cold, and try to grasp the language of imperatives around me. There is a sense of protest in their voices. I watch couples articulating pleas using words still for the most part alien to me. A young man sits alone in the corner. He had married for love. She had married for status and money, and now he looks like he has already run out of dreams. Outside, passers-by on the snow-sludge-stained streets cross themselves right to left before the golden cupolas. Not once, but four times. I counted.

At the close of each day, I would make my way dutifully to the Pyatkin restaurant. Located on the main street, Pyatkin is housed in a columned, classical style building that speaks a Tolstoyesque charm. Patrician ladies can be seen entering the building in impressive furs. Inside, it is like a nineteenth century pre-revolution Russian aristocrat's living room. Diners are surrounded by giant silver samovars, Prussian art, dog-eared books and gramophones. There are elaborately patterned rugs. Clocks chatter in the hallway. The damask, floral table cloths and upholstery match the curtains and their chintz pelmets. I would browse the menu weighing up Tolstoy's free will and necessity. Around me are shed reflections of nobility: an opulent, bloated by Empire décor with a menu to match. A miscellany of delicious fish soups (*solyanka, ukha* and *shchi*), a dozen different types of *pelmeni*, caviar (pike, salmon, sturgeon), *kvass, mors*, a long list of beers and vodkas and home-made rye bread. For he who likes plain food, there can be few things better than a Russian fish plate of herring and salmon with bread and gherkins washed down with ice cold vodka.

I came here each evening. Each evening, I would be greeted with the same bemused smile as a gun-dog pushed past waitresses dressed in intricately embroidered *sarafans*, anxious to take up his place by the window. Head rotating left and right watching his four-legged peers pass on the snowy pavements, Stan focused on the goings-on outside whilst I wrote my notes and snacked on *zakuski* of cured fish and pickled vegetables. Such *zakuski* were always to be found in the pantry of any nineteenth century Russian gentleman worth his salt; they would be served to travelers staying at the house whose arrival time was not known. Following a surfeit of fish, my dinner would end with cheese cake and a cup of *ivan chai* (willow herb tea). Somehow, this habit became immediately ingrained. As I collected my things and untied Stan from the gilt bronze Russian Gueridon table, one of the waitresses would rush over to see me off the premises. A tiny Orthodox cross with its triple transom hangs around her throat; she wears a frown of judicious insight as she inspects my attire. She would make a point of telling me how to dress up for the cold, making sure I did not venture outside before having my hat on. She would cast a glance at my shoes to make sure they were suitably polished before allowing me to leave the restaurant, even though they were about to be caked in slush or *kasha* (porridge) as the Russians call it.

On my last day, I explored the other side of Nizhny. This side of the city feels gritty, down-at-heel and unruly. The occasional stray dog follows us through streets of proud melancholy on the peninsula where the Volga flows into the Oka. The embankment is pitted with cranes. Here was to be found the fruits of some eccentric urban planning; a bricolaged landscape of glass and steel shopping precincts, Soviet housing, baroque churches and wide-open spaces serving no obvious function. The nineteenth century Alexander Nevsky cathedral is oddly juxtaposed with the new football stadium built for the 2018 World Cup. The intention was to plant lots of trees to make the awkward juxtaposition look a little less austere, but thus far the area around the stadium remains an empty concrete car park. An incoherent plaza of splintering pavements.

Beneath a surge of spires, tiered Orthodox crosses and golden cupolas, I enter the hallowed, indispensable silence; the spiritual warmth. The blessed sixty-ton bell begins to peal: I am reminded of how might and virtue reigned in this land during the time of Alexander Nevsky. Except for the occasional warden removing burnt candles, the fire of God's love, I am the only person here. I walk under arresting domes of fresco paintings depicting the transfiguration of life.

Following the defeat of the Swedish invaders in the thirteenth century, Nevsky foresaw his own death and took the Great Schema. He was in this life, but no longer of it. He embraced the moral code of divinity, but once he passed from the outer to the inner world could probably no longer express the grace he had found to others. He had entered the world of binaries – divinity and impurity, black and white, godly and ungodly. Nevsky sought to follow in the shadow of Christ and understood that holiness is not a theoretical idea.

I return to the entrance to buy a candle from the lady at the candle stand:

'I like the silence', the head scarved lady says with a smile.

'This is life. Our silent relationship between God and what is intimate to us'. Her shoulders have the attitude of lament; her eyes tinged with melancholy.

I reflect on her words. The true spiritual experience transcends human language. We struggle to express the profound mysteries of God through words. She hands me the candle:

'You like our cathedral?', she continues.

'The cathedral was closed by Soviet authorities in 1930 and not re-opened until 1992', she whispers.

'You see that icon there?', she points to a small icon on the left-hand side of the nave.

'My mother hid that icon in her house for over sixty years'.

She crosses herself, smiles and says 'thanks be to God'. Her pious manner is propaganda for sainthood. Elderly *babushka*, the girders of Russian society, risked their lives by hiding the icons in their attics. Few icon painters survived persecution from the KGB in that long, troubled century:

'My grandfather was arrested and taken away in 1937', continues Irina as her glance reaches mine. 'It was September 21. It was dawn and my grandmother and him were reading the Akathist to our most holy lady Theotokos when there was a knock at the door. The men dressed in green tunics and brass buttons started by checking documents and their passports, but then they found his vestments hidden at the back of the wardrobe'. She looks up at the fresco of Christ in the cupola and says 'God save us'. She turns to me and slowly nods as if imparting a truism: 'he was part of the unlucky generation'. The past keeps beating within her like an ageing heart. There is always a sense of struggle here.

I thank her, place the candle in front of the once hidden icon of the Mother of God, reflect on the beauty of this sacred place of angelic visions and take my leave.

* * *

Outside – the tyranny of noise – sleet has become swirling snow. Dogs bark. Men smoke cigarettes. A few beggars in dog voices huddle on the steps. My reminiscence is broken; my thoughts ransacked. The birds are returning home, and it is time for me too to go to the hotel, collect my things and make my way to the railway station. I am on the 17:43 to Moscow.

Stan in Nizhny Novgorod

The Night Train to Kazan

An Orthodox Christmas

A BARE-CHESTED MAN GAZES out of the window watching the queue of passengers that wait on the platform to have their travel documents inspected. Content his entourage have made it onto the train, he walks towards me down the extremely narrow corridor that runs alongside the four-berth couchette compartments. His stomach is impressive and sufficiently large that it proves impossible to pass in the corridor even if we both stand sideways and breathe in. Nonetheless, he tries to squeeze past. Anxious to avoid getting *coincé* amidst layers of white fat, I retreat back down the corridor under his smoky breath. Poker-faced, he passes me with a sulky grunt not wishing to see the funny side of the encounter.

We have just boarded the night train to Kazan and everybody is anxious to find their compartment and get settled in for the evening. It takes thirteen hours from Moscow which is a relatively short journey in Russian terms. I say 'we'. I am traveling with my two-year-old spaniel, Stan. Traveling with a dog comes with its challenges, but he is warmly received everywhere we go. When traveling on the night train with a dog you have to buy the whole compartment, i.e. four couchettes instead of one. Families of six on their way to Kazan to celebrate Orthodox Christmas on January 7 are jammed into the cramped, adjacent carriages of the same size. Endless parcels of tin-foil wrapped homemade food are unpacked and shared. Sprawled out across the leather seats with Stan at my knees and the leftovers of the New Year's Eve caviar on my lap, I feel like a pre-revolutionary Russian aristocrat in comparison even if these second-class compartments are rather basic. There are no gilded dining cars with their sounds of shaken glass or tuxedoed men sipping Bellinis. Instead, a long queue of men in slippers soon forms at the one socket to charge their mobile phones.

There is a groaning and creaking. The train lurches and the dimmed compartment lights brighten. The frenzy of Moscow floats away from us as we trundle east. I close the compartment door and secure the privacy that is the romance of train travel. For us foreigners at least, these night trains have a Soviet nostalgic appeal. Tea is brought to you in a fancy metal tea glass holder – enabling you not to burn your fingers – called a *podstakannik* by a stern-faced conductor (*provodnitsa*) whose tiny half-compartment lies at the end of the corridor. Two *provodnitsa* are responsible for each carriage and their tasks might include: making and delivering tea, sorting out the passengers' bedlinen, maintaining the coal-heated *samovar*, collecting and returning train tickets and giving out information on the vast train timetable which covers seven time zones but that all runs on Moscow time. Train journeys can take up to a week in Russia and it makes sense to be on good terms with your *provodnitsa* as they not only bring you tea but take away your travel documents until you leave the train. For those people traveling alone, they will spend the next few days in overflowing *vagon* sharing everything with complete strangers.

We edge slowly through the blackened Russian countryside in the thick of the night. Eager to see something other than Soviet era pre-fabricated tower blocks, my forehead rests on the cold window. All I can see is the transparent reflection of my own features. The swaying carriage and rhythmic shudder of the train soon send Stan and I to sleep. I awake shortly before midnight. The *provodnitsa* knocks on the *kupe* door. The train has stopped. All is silent. We will be here for ten minutes and I take Stan out onto the unmade and unlit Zhivagoesque platform where the latest snow swirls in the wind. The snow is deep here. A few late-night hawkers sell a variety of Christmas decorations: baubles with embossed images of Putin and hanging *matryoshka*. Back on the train, I awake in the morning to the sound of the familiar rattling of the *podstakannik* being delivered to my fellow passengers up and down the corridor. This is a nation of tea-drinkers and my co-travelers seem to drink endless cups of tea. I open the blind and before me are snowy forests of birch and the occasional near-abandoned, ramshackle village of piecemeal dachas with their characteristic high mansard roofs. The villages recede into the distance and we idle into the sidings at Kazan.

Sitting on what was the historic Siberian trade route – an artery that connected Siberia with Moscow –, Kazan remains a fascinating transit of cultures. It is particularly conspicuous in its show-casing of all things Tatar. Tatar flags fly ceremoniously across the city; the main thoroughfare (Bauman St) comprises a strip of Tatar restaurants, souvenir stands and shops selling local foods. Tatar cuisine is quite distinct from Russian and all manner of fares are on display: *chak-chak* (honey-drenched sweet pastry balls); *kazylyk* (air-dried horse meat sausage); *kaklagan gaz* (air-dried goose); bear meat snacks and boxes of *talkysh kaleve* (pyramids of threaded honey and sugar). At the end of Bauman St., the kremlin houses the city's architectural splendors including the Cathedral of the Annunciation juxtaposed to the Kul Sharif Mosque which at the time of its completion was the largest mosque in Europe. Inside, the prayer hall is a plain hexagon of marble. In one of the corners, a cleric sits in a glass paneled cubicle reading from the Koran as Chinese tourists video him on their Smartphones. Nestled between the cathedral and the mosque is the tiered and notably leaning Söyembikä tower. Its history is intriguing and very Russian. It is said that Ivan the Terrible fell in love with a woman and built what was at the time the highest building in Kazan as a symbol of his love. She climbed up to the top and threw herself off.

Beyond the kremlin, Kazan is a mix of attractive parks, crumbling mansions, neo-classical theatres and frozen lakes. In the parks, decorated with statues of prize-winning mathematicians, young newly-weds hang locked padlocks on the bridges as a token of their love. Having been dragged by a spaniel through all the parks, I warm up in cozy cafés and make conversation with strangers: Turks, Uzbeks, Tatars, Russians and Ukrainians. It is here that I discover the delights of green *borscht* (sorrel, not beetroot based) and *echpochmak* (a kind of small triangular Cornish pasty) whilst discussing the notable people of Kazan: poets, Soviet fencers, cellists, models and the wife of Salvador Dali.

Satisfied that I have exhausted the attractions of the city center, I decide to take a taxi to Raifa Bogoroditsky monastery. The monastery lies in the forest beyond the city and has served believers more or less since the sixteenth century. As with almost all the monasteries, it was closed after the revolution and used as a prison camp for political prisoners. With the Krushchev Thaw, the camp was closed in the 1950s. The monastery fell into disrepair and was only reopened in 1991. We approach it under a louring sky. It is January 6, Christmas Eve for Orthodox Christians and the traffic is heavy. Normally a place of silence and solitude, the monastery has attracted today (unsurprisingly) a heaving throng of worshippers inching towards the cathedral under a leaden sky. Raifa is a complex of attractive temples and bell towers. The semantron and then the bells – blessed, consecrated and icons of the voice of God – ring out across the wintry woods. The Orthodox bell *is* a voice, and it should be loud because God is omnipotent.

A number of cats which have made their home here scatter amongst the crowds. Queues of head-scarved women snake around the cathedral, waiting to kiss the Our Lady of Georgia icon. God is patient and forgiving. The nave fills up with saintly reverence. The women move like chess pieces between relics lit by lamps and candles, kissing the glass and then quickly rubbing away the mark. A silent, congested train of people in the narthex fill out prayer slips, writing the names of the living (red slip) and the dead (black slip) that they want the priest to pray for. Keen to escape the crowds, I go to the adjacent temple. A clowder of cats skulk on the steps. Inside, a male choir of *basso profundo* rehearse the low notes in preparation for the All-Night Vigil tonight. Meandering melodies spiral forth. At the entrance to the chapel, I meet Dmitry, the monk responsible for the cats. In return for looking after the rodents, the cats are fed and receive blessings as he walks amongst the ancient buildings sprinkling holy water. 'We do this every day. They are very blessed cats', and with a laugh rejoins his fellow choir members.

I queue to visit the tiniest chapel with room for just seven people, and then leave the monastery complex under the onomatopoeic sound of the bells. The harmony is enchanting and exclamatory. I pass the impressive ice sculptures of shrines and make my way back to Kazan. With his flowing beard and hair tied in a ponytail, my driver, Sergei, has the look of an Orthodox priest. He is jovial and speaks with a booming voice. A pride in Orthodoxy can be ascertained. He is in his mid-forties, divorced, and has spent his whole life in Kazan. Garrulous and thick-set, he clearly devoted little time to controlling that middle-aged corpulence to which he was predisposed but is nonetheless full of Orthodox virtues: humility, patience and fear of God. A prayer rope hangs from the rear-view mirror. He tells me how he was baptized at home in secret during Soviet times:

'Yes, even then they managed to keep alive the faith in the hearts of the people', he continues.

'My case was doubly difficult. My father was a member of the Party and so my mother had to keep my baptism secret from him too. Only when he died did my mother reveal that I had been baptized on the kitchen table!' In a spate of excited words, he tells me how happy he is that the Christian faith in Russia found its footing again.

A glance at the Navigator app on his phone and Sergei says with a deep sigh that the *propka* (traffic jam) will result in a long journey. A ten-mile traffic jam awaits ahead. But he has a plan, and asks my permission to take the scenic route. I am only too pleased. Sergei has a twinkle in his eye and tries to disguise a half-grin. Coming off the main road, he takes us through small villages comprising a mish-mash of worn dachas pieced together with whatever materials were available. The dacha lined streets soon become grey suburbs of totalitarian architecture and built ideology – Soviet housing blocks with their cold war narratives huddling on the verges of the Volga. We weave between ruts and pot-holes. Sergei's half-grin becomes a chortle as we turn off into an unmade track littered with rusting machinery. The track drops sharply and the car meanders on the ice. A few chassis-reshaping thumps and then we are driving rather suddenly on the frozen Volga River. Beaming, he looks at me and says *eto Rossiya* ('only in Russia').

Clinging perhaps to a nomadic ancestry, groups of Turkic looking men fish through the ice. They seem a little surprised by our ungainly entrance. It is -4 degrees, one of the mildest Russian winters on record and my eyes are fixed on the patches of grey ice. Flashbacks of conversations with the Inuit about the dangers of the thin grey ice race through my mind. We both give a nervous laugh as the Navigator map on his iPhone spins in confusion. This is the first time I have been taken off-road in an Uber. We follow a well-worn track across the ice and traverse the smooth, frozen river with minimal fuss. A few grinds of the gearbox, up an icy embankment and before we know it we are again amongst the golden onion-domes and minarets of the Kazan kremlin.

Sergei and I share a grin, and perhaps a sense of adventure. He drops me off in the city center and holds out his hand: 'I think I will go to Vigil tonight. I need some smells and bells. Haha', he chuckles. 'Perhaps you would like to join me? This should be something beautiful. I can pick you up hotel at about 11pm?'

* * *

Sergei enters the monastery in that proprietorial way that is permitted to regular church-goers. Tradition and the love of God brings the worshippers together. A panoply of beautiful expressions of obedience leaves me immersed in the Vigil; the rituals are embodied. For much of the service, the monastery is candle lit only; melismatic, liturgical singing appears from nowhere. A solemn beauty. The Litany of Fervent Supplication seems to float above us in the near complete darkness. Night is all around us. The uninterrupted prayer purifies the heart. Candles lit before the icons whisper to one another as wicks drown in their own wax pools. The faithful wander in, kiss and venerate the central icon and then join the huddle of cowled ladies. I feel like I am glued to the ground in awe but Sergei walks around greeting fellow worshippers, lighting candles and kissing icons. The sanctuary is being censed – the spirit of God moves through the void at the beginning of the world. The deacon intones the Great Litany, leading a prayer for travelers by land, by sea and by air. God broods over us constantly and is refuge for the weary; salvation for those assailed by unspeakable thoughts.

Even if we have escaped the world of time (the Vigil comprises both Matins and Vespers and thus encompasses the *whole of time*), readings from the Psalter are intermingled with a multitude of stichera, sessional hymns and troparia that have lasted apparently for a full four hours. There is no rush to achieve results here. It is a time of observance and that is all. I have been standing silently, anchored to the stone floor 'keeping watch', shifting now and then weight from one leg to another. Everything aches: shoulders, legs, neck. Crippling contractions in the lower back. Cramp in my right foot. To Sergei's amusement, I stumble out of the church – spiritually enraptured and enlightened, but physically broken. He pats me on the back: 'no pain, no gain!'

Babushkas with looks of eternal perdition and legs of steel cross themselves one last time and take their leave. It is Christmas morning. Sergei and I wish one another 'Merry Christmas':

'You see, despite over seventy years of persecution, the beauty of the Orthodox liturgy remains', says Sergei with a contented smile. We drive back to Kazan. The night sky above us is lit up with the glowing cascade of the Milky Way. Faintly heard *chansons* that sing of prison life and repentance trickle from the radio.

A wintry day in Kazan with The Kul Sharif Mosque in the background

Chapter 2: Latvia

'We are imprisoned in the realm of language and cannot escape'
(Ludwig Wittgenstein)

Mr. Jansons

A visit to a café in Riga

THE CAFÉ WAS CALLED Sienna. It occupied a prominent position on a street of Eisenstein designed art nouveau *façades*: sphinxes, cherubs and steles of peacock watch you as you saunter down the street, head helicoptering in the breeze to capture their expressions. The eyes of gargoyles beneath kidney-shaped windows inspect the guests as they enter the mansions and ascend their elaborately decorated spiral staircases. Isaiah Berlin lived down the road at the top of one these ornamental snail staircases and wrote about concepts of liberty.

Entering the café, a shopkeeper's bell tinkles and a Viennese style *Herr Ober* appears immediately, bidding the guests welcome. The café is of a different era entirely. With its faded elegance, it feels more like a late imperial living room. French empire-style chandeliers hang from the ceiling and the walls are lined with worn-around-the-edges Biedermeier sofas. Ladies dressed in pink and wearing cloche hats catch up on the news in crisp Russian. Freshly powdered dames appear from behind sienna-colored curtains to rejoin them. People come here to embrace nostalgia and escape the world of time, it seems.

The waiter – let's call him Mr. Jansons – weaves between nineteenth century furniture, taking ladies' coats and hanging them up in the walnut-veneered armoire. The couple from Sweden have entered his domain of old-fashioned etiquette and timeless sophistication. His deportment is irreproachable; his manners impeccable, and perhaps suggestive of the same period as the furniture. He seems flustered as they move towards the recently vacated corner table. He has not had a chance to prepare the table and escorts them instead to two well-padded *fauteuils* whilst he makes the necessary preparations. Everything had to be just so. Behind them, a serious-looking Norwegian massages the bridge of his nose. He watches the blond man, and wondering if he is one of his countrymen, starts to whisper to the lady sat opposite him. To his left sit two cuff-linked *bon chic bon genre* French gentlemen discussing architecture: Gustav Klimt, Otto Wagner, Adolf Loos. The Latvians speak more quietly than the Russians, but we should not entertain stereotypes. The Swedish couple recognize the Latvian phonemic vowel length, but only understand the odd word. With the exception of the Russian woman sitting close to the front door and whose grating, metallic voice becomes impossible to ignore, the people in the café speak in hushed tones as if they were in a library or a church. Foreign voices mingle with the refreshingly refined sound of clinking porcelain, and the hours drift by.

The table prepared, Jansons beckons them to their seats in front of the window, partially hidden by stacks of coffee table books on art, photography and fashion. Faded oil paintings on the adjacent wall are reflected on the surface of the window. Standing dutifully behind the antique cake stand trolley, he introduces them to the cakes in Russian, Latvian and English. If he were asked to do it in German, Polish and Hungarian, one suspects it would pose few problems. He takes his time with the descriptions, almost anthropomorphizing the perfect, glazed desserts. There are éclairs, crème brûlées, Latvian cheesecake, Sachertorte and much more. The young Swedish man orders Earl Grey impérial and a crème brûlée. The anti-coffee chain par excellence, the porcelain cups are of all different styles and designs and of exceptional quality.

As if he were handling a precious stone, he opens the transparent roll top dessert trolley and with hallmarked silver pastry tongs prizes the desired puddings. Anxious not to distract the newly arrived guest and cause a spillage, Jansons tangos behind him with bent knee at a respectable distance as he pours the tea. The guest is unsure whether he has trespassed into one of Jansons' responsibilities. 'It is perfectly alright, Sir. It happens occasionally', he imagines him saying to himself. Attentive to detail, solicitous of others, Jansons flutters between the customers, taking orders in Russian, Latvian and English.

Burdened by propriety and enslaved in his principles, Mr. Jansons waits alone on the customers. He could not risk sharing the tasks or losing control. The risk would be existential for the requirements of his position have determined his character entirely. His duty is to his customers, many of whom he has served for a score of years or more. He would fetch their coats, take their orders, deliver their teas, coffees and cakes, take payment, hold the door for them and escort them off the premises with a half-smile. This role he inhabited to the utmost. He would know the names of many of his customers, but would never cross the public-private threshold, preferring to address everybody as Sir or Madam and their equivalents in a multitude of languages. What mattered to Jansons was professionalism. Indeed, he had devoted his professional life to Sienna. He had become wedded to the anachronistic values and social system that the café represented. He had become Sienna. Without Jansons, there was no Sienna.

Brought up by his mother on the Baltic coast on sprats, eels, flounders, lamprey and cod, Jansons was an only child whose upbringing sheltered him from the more rude parts of life. Unmarried, he had known though the coils of love and passion. He lived in a small, understated flat in an unfashionable part of Riga. Once his mother died, he was left alone with the mists of his constantly running inner monologues: 'should I call her?; should I marry?; should I live out this life alone?' In the winter evenings, stretched out on the cabriole-legged *chaise longue* and surrounded by inherited furniture that was refreshingly of another era, he would heave a heavy, Port-fueled nostalgic sigh. This was the life his mother had always wanted for him. A life lived out amongst silver toast racks, wine cisterns, engraved pitchers and chiming clocks with complicated French movements. She had wanted him to escape from the tragedy of modern furniture to the tastes and faded elegance of an earlier century; a world of French doors, ornate carvings and neglected paintings.

He had worked the carved rosewood tables at Sienna for twenty-seven years and had learnt his trade from a Mr. Edgars. Edgars was devoted to Sienna. Whilst serving a Latvian honey cake to a customer, Edgars had collapsed and died from a heart-attack sending the cake flying into the customer's lap. 'Jansons, the honey cake, the honey cake', were to be his dying words. From that day on, Jansons had worked alone at Sienna, believing that Edgars was irreplaceable and that nobody else could measure up to his former employer's commitment and professionalism. He lived with a fear that tasks would not be undertaken quite correctly. Edgars had taught Jansons how to treat one's customers with the utmost respect and courtesy, being obliging but never too close and personal. No matter how congenial *gospodin* X or Y may seem, no matter how embracing *gospoda* Z's small-talk may be, one should always maintain a social distance, peripheral to any conversation and should never speak more than necessary. One should respond to questions and then retreat silently into the background to allow the guests to talk. 'Remember, Jansons, you are a shadow that speaks. Nothing more. Nothing less', Edgars would say.

It is with this in mind that one damp November morning with the rain splashing the parquet, *she* entered Sienna. It was half a generation ago that they last met. They had been on-off lovers. Beneath the slender iron columns of the bay window opposite and amidst a motley of sculptured femme fatales, she had been watching Jansons drift effortlessly between the customers. Nothing had changed. He had not changed. Slightly grey at the temples, he wore the same expression of solemn duty. Nervously, she approached the café. She had to speak to him one last time. She was looking for some kind of closure. The rain raked down the lane. She collapsed her umbrella; bulging raindrops lined up down the rib of the umbrella landed on her clavicle. She adjusted her hairpins, breathed deeply and gently pushed open the café door. Jansons cocks his head over his right shoulder to acknowledge the guest. Recognizing her immediately, his cheeks turn the color of beet; the Lomonosov porcelain coffee cups rattle and clink nervously in his shaking hand as they struggle to maintain their place in the saucers' depressions. Hot tea and citrus peel slop into the saucer:

'I am terribly sorry. Forgive me. I don't know what came over me, Sir', pleads Jansons to the gentleman ensconced in the armchair.

Looking up from his book, the gentleman swivels round to inspect the woman responsible for the spillage and who skulks awkwardly at the entrance. His glance returns to Jansons whose face has gone from beet-colored to crimson. 'No problem. It is perfectly fine', the seated gentleman insists.

The elegant woman standing at the entrance clasps her dripping umbrella, fixes her eyes on Jansons and attempts a smile. She unbuttons her rain coat to reveal a mid-length pencil skirt and single-breasted jacket with notched collar. The café is full, its regular customers indulging on elevensies, sharing newspapers and exchanging the latest gossip in sunken tones:

'Kaspars. Hello', says the newly arrived lady in a dulcet tone. There is a long, pregnant pause. Sienna's coffee and tea drinkers look at one another. With furrowed brows, a few whisper quizzically 'Kaspars, Kaspars...'

Unsteady on his feet and with sweating palms, Jansons clears his throat repeatedly and gingerly walks towards the lady with a faltering gait. He struggles to maintain his air of unruffled dignity. The conversation in the café has fallen silent. Everybody looks at Jansons, speculating who this woman might be. The last time he saw her she stood freshly alighted on a busy station platform in the swollen shadows of late afternoon. Her smoky eyes tinged with a vague iridescence swept the platform in search of Jansons.

Jansons' throat feels oddly dry. Scraping around to find some phlegm, he struggles to turn his thoughts into words: 'Erm…we are rather busy at the moment, Madam. Might I take the lady's coat or perhaps you would care to return later when we are a bit…erh…quieter?':

'Kaspars. It is me. Lilja. Please. It is me. Can we talk?', she urges.

'Talk', thought Kaspars to himself. 'Talk'. He gave her a troubled glance. He moved uneasily on his feet. Can there be a language without deceit?, he wondered. Is the falsehood in words or things? Kaspars knew how words could be conspiratorial, how language could not be perfectly expressed in things themselves. He had told himself so many times that 'inner speech is our only true self', it marched like a banner across his mind.

Bemused onlookers rapidly assemble romantic narratives in their heads. One of them starts talking about the 'dialectic of love'. She did not care to make a scene. Jansons rediscovers the dignity that Edgars, that pillar of probity, had taught him. For a moment, no longer the liminal figure, he straightens his back with the manner of someone who wasn't going to allow himself to be put upon and raises his chin: 'Madam, allow me to take your coat. I might perhaps find you a place next to the chiffonier'.

In the hope of dissipating Jansons' embarrassment which everybody was beginning to share, the Swedish couple gather their things and offer their seat to the standing lady. Her awkward presence adjacent to silent tables had ground the flow of conversation at Sienna to a halt. Even the un-flagging monologue of the Russian woman with the tiny voice had ceased with the force of surprise. Jansons' old lover had come to deliver a message, it seemed, something rather important, something that could simply not wait any longer. She takes the Swedish man's seat and in doing so, the café-goers' conversation starts gradually to potter along again.

The young couple move towards the door, confident that they have diffused the situation:

'Thank you, Sir. Thank you, Madam', says Jansons, still a little flustered.

He retrieves their coats from the armoire, helps them into their macs and escorts them efficiently to the door. He opens the door; the sound of trams creaking around the city fills the room. The road rumbles under their panting weight. Rustling leaves race into the entrance. Hunched over, passersby turn up their collars under bloated rain-clouds. Fiddling with the buttons on their coats, the couple stand briefly on the threshold to the café trying to make sense of the goings-on but it was alas impossible for the exchanges that mattered were non-verbal:

'Mr. Jansons, Mr. Jansons', shouted the woman who had occupied the Swede's seat. She had risen with the manner of somebody intending to address the café-dwellers en masse.

'Mr. Jansons…I wanted, I wanted to…'. No longer the introvert, the woman appeared confident, but then her sudden burst of confidence subsided as quickly as it had arisen. 'I…erh…I…Mr. Jansons, may I have a cup of tea please?'

Relieved and smiling, Jansons says 'but, of course, madam'. The tiny voiced Russian by the window who had finally stopped speaking, giggles and offers 'love is the death of duty'.

Pleased to have brought about some kind of puzzling equilibrium, the couple take their leave and embrace the fresh Baltic air. The puddled streets glisten under the street lamps; the flamboyant friezes and window entablatures have become grey in late afternoon. They walk briskly through the wet streets and then begin to jog a little as they see their tram screech and squeal into the corner. The doors of the blue and white carriage spring open with the energy of a jack-in-the-box. With a firm grasp of the cold iron hand rails, they climb the steps and take their seats. Single seats line the left-hand side of the carriage, double seats the right. Lost in introspection, an elderly man mumbles to himself acknowledging his reflection on the damp window. The contemplative soul is worth knowing. Behind them two pairs of raucous Russian boys, shouting and gesticulating, make a great to-do about their exploits out on the town the previous evening. They get off at the national theatre stop, and the remaining few passengers are left listening to the clang of the electric tram and the sound of the rain pecking against the windows.

Back in the café, the last few remaining guests gathered their things, thanked Mr. Jansons and one-by-one went in the direction of the tram stop. At last, Lilja and Kaspars were alone. She had missed his dignity. She liked the way he always wanted to serve her, the way he paid attention to every word she said. The rain continued to tap on the window. The couple spoke in Latvian. Occasionally, his face tightened as he appraised the situation. She stood and looked him in the eye:

'Kaspars, I came to tell you that I am getting married'. A short silence ensued. He turned away to digest the news in a dignified manner. He fixed his professional demeanor and only then returned her glance:

'I am happy for your Lilja. Happy that your thoughts have become things'. She clasped his hand. A touch of reassurance. He felt as if he never had enough words as if language was always playing catch-up with reality, but he would not surrender his emotions:

'Thank you, Kaspars. Thank you. I just wanted you to know. And I wanted you to know that you can find what you are looking for too. You mustn't fear anything, Kaspars. Fear is just inverted faith'.

She opened the café door. It tinkled one last time.

'Goodbye Kaspars. Goodbye'. There was a look of sorrow in her eyes.

Inside Sienna in Riga, Latvia

Chapter 3: The Faroes

'The writer must be able to revel and roll in the abundance of words; he must know not only the direct but the secret power of a word. There are overtones and undertones to a word, and lateral echoes too' (Knut Hamsun)

Listening to the Faroese

A visit to the church at Sandvík,
the Faroe Islands

SUNDAY MORNING. THE HOUSES are sleeping. From a distant window, a spinster can be seen sidling into her sitting room with spools of wool. Sheep dogs walk the static streets with perfect freedom, sniffing at strangers, chasing their own shadows. No owner in sight. On the hill, unattended children play hopscotch, flitting like butterflies and sucking on gobstoppers. They shout a volley of consonants and produce for their imaginary companions fantasy dialogues of non-words in a covert, private speech. Doors to their homes are left ajar; radios can be heard crackling in nearby sitting rooms. A fizz of static. Through an open, Prussian blue-curtained window, I hear a woman singing. Her voice is mystical, belonging with the gulls that are catapulted across the sky in front of her. Her broken words become lost in the wind.

A retired trawler man with one eye on the sea saunters up the hill to the church at Sandvík, past laundry hanging from lines, still wet from yesterday's drizzle. We chat briefly about the weather and he points to the clouds pillowing on the hill, throwing a pall over the valley. 'Bad weather. But, soon it will be gone', he says with unexpected cheeriness. His eyes peer towards the slippery shore where a father and son are crabbing in the drizzle. Further along the shore line, hooded crows with quarter-grins drop mollusks on the bare rocks from a great height and a brace of Eider ducks brood in the fjord. Their pantomime 'oohing' seems almost satirical.

Once in the church, two female church wardens with shingled hair and drawn-on eyebrows approach me; their tobacco-colored eyes are full of proud memories of events that have taken place in this building. Huddled in the narrow nave, they summarize the church's impressive history in excitable, arm-waving vignettes, producing piles of drawings and photographs of the church in its earlier guises. With rouged cheeks, their eyes fix on me. They stand slightly too close, breathing out in fetid bursts. Their legs are netted in veins; their puffy fingers weighed down with jewelry. We talk about the local dialect and the lost words blown away into the ether of the tunnel. 'Oh, you must speak to Einar', they say. He remembers the old words. Then a few more residents soldier in, and our party breaks up.

No more than seventy-five people live in Sandvík today. But, I am told there are just a few children. The chaotic, high pitched collective twitter has almost fallen silent. But writers have lived here, and sculptors have left their mark. Down by the shore, a Hans Pauli Olsen sculpture of Sigmundur Brestisson, *hin seinasta ferðin* ('the final journey') reminds us of the first Faroese to convert to the Christian faith. 'Sigmundur Brestisson introduced Christianity to the Faroe Islands in 999' offers one of the church wardens. A polite smile flits across her face. 'The pagan, Tróndur í Gøtu, attacked Sigmundur one night at his yard in Skúvoy, an island further north' she continues. 'Sigmundur fled by swimming to Sandvík, here on the island of Suðuroy, a distance of nine miles. The *Færeyinga saga* tells us that the exhausted Sigmundur was killed by a local Suðuroy farmer when he arrived on the Sandvík shore', she says.

The smiling wardens apologize that the congregation will be small today, but I like it this way. I warm to the smallness of everything here. It is a microcosm of well-being. And the words seem to have a greater impact if there are fewer to absorb them. There are fifteen anoraked souls dotted amongst the pews, organizing their thoughts and deleting their transgressions. Charcoal-haired descendants of shipwrecks and seventeenth century pirates fondle well-thumbed psalters. A couple whisper to one another on the pew behind me. I think to myself how their scrunching words are made for life on the choppy sea. I listen to the hushed *dj* and *ch* sounds colliding with one another, merging with the wind thumping on the glass. I wait for the service to start and watch the shadows slide down the walls.

We are startled slightly by the metallic clang of the bell; the call to prayer still means something on these islands. When the bells toll and knell, the pews are sometimes packed with purple-faced people listening to the peal. With so many people lost at sea, the significance of the church has never really waned in such tightly-knit communities. And it is here, on these small mid-Atlantic islands shaped by weather, that you feel as if there is something bigger than you, something close and over-arching. It is always there, the proximity of nature, the proximity of fate.

Two tousle-haired stragglers in soiled cardigans squeeze past the priest who pulls on the bell-rope. The final additions to the congregation take up their seats on the pew at the back of the church where children would have once played hide-and-seek. One picks his teeth with a grass-stem. The other extracts the dirt from under his nails and flicks it onto the leather hassocks. It is unusual for a priest to hold the service in this tiny *bygd* ('village'), and there is no guarantee there will be an organist either. At a church service in neighboring Hvalba, a couple of miles to the south and on the other side of the tunnel, the organist and his boyfriend had recently come from Tórshavn – a two-hour boat ride; the church-goers gossiped about them in the weeks that followed. But irrespective of whether a priest, organist or neither turns up, the islanders get by just fine. These Lutheran services are designed so that any lay-preacher can introduce the hymns and knows exactly where to read from the Bible. The congregation committed the liturgy to memory long ago. The bachelor twins who lived in identical bedrooms in the village of Sumba also on the island of Suðuroy told me how they knew the entire Book of Psalms in Faroese (off by heart). As children, they spent several hours a day singing. The Bible and Book of Psalms were more or less the only written material that generation had in their own language.

There is a pause among the muffled voices. Jugular bulging beneath his Lutheran ruff, the priest strolls up the aisle with a knowing smile. Half-child, half-man, he carries a desiccated and punctured leather briefcase. The ruff gives him an aristocratic air and conjures up images of early seventeenth century ceremonial paintings in ancient dining halls. His eyes are glassy, his face pale. A poker-faced organist sits behind a wooden door adjacent to the font, having delivered the opening prayer in a tired monotone. Then, the priest begins to speak. He speaks with a delicate authority. Between the priest's deliberate pauses, you can hear the raindrops peck against the leaded windows. He ascends the pulpit. His voice is lavish – velvety and smooth, but penetrating. It girdles heaven. A sense of finality falls upon each word, so that the congregation has a chance to ponder the suspended meaning. He stands, yoked to the lectern; the forefingers of his fish-scaled hands grip the wood and bulge crimson with blood. The priest paints a pictorial language with his arms. Then, his hands travel back to the lectern and his fingers march slow time on the oak. I analyze the architecture and capillaries of his syntax, the timing of his syllables. He pronounces the words as if each were bursting with profound meaning, as if the language belonged to him. The words twist and turn. The joy of hearing the pulse of the Faroese language is partly what brings me here. The vowels sweep around the curvy lanes, and the consonants squelch in the mud.

The Faroese love to hear the spoken word, the local voice, the figures of speech that are shared by so few. They sing Faroese songs morning and night, compose cadenzas and remember ballads that paint pictures of seditious soldiers, bloody battles and buckled men. On the radio, they talk about the conscription of Faroese metaphors, nouns dressing as verbs and how they can 'bend' their language. 'We are fond of the declinations', I remember one of the bachelor twins telling me repeatedly. The Faroese share an intimacy with their language, playing with the sounds to make new words that have an acoustic, poetic appeal.

It is the sounds of the Faroese language (so different from Danish which all Faroese also speak) that for many spells home; an acoustic togetherness celebrated in the church, on the radio and in the community halls. I remember when I first fell for the letters: the ø and å had somehow an ancient, mythical allure. They felt like orthographic relics from a forgotten era of oral epic poetry. I wanted to know their sounds. It was the same with the coins. I can remember as a child examining the Danish kroner (the currency used in the Faroes) coins with holes in them, imagining the holes representing the small circles over the letter 'å'.

I am half-listening to the sermon, and the words are more sounds than meaning. The beauty of half-listening is the appreciation of the physicality of the voice. The tone comes before the word. I register the rhythm, the volume, the contours. And, then the words. They sit on the outer edge of my consciousness. They are like small acoustic parcels that bounce around, not quite settling in my memory. And then come the semantics. By dint of persistent concentration, my mind moves from hearing the words as music to actually digesting their meaning.

Here, language is shaped by the actions and events of people living in the landscape. After the service, I sit chatting to my neighbor about the Faroese language. *samgonga* ('communications, alliance, union') whispers the short-haired woman with curt consonants next to me. It comes from the drive of sheep undertaken jointly by owners of adjoining parts of the field. 'We shape our language ourselves', she insists. 'From the way we live'. We like to play with the language. There is a pause. 'You like music?', she asks. 'Yes, well, *tonleik* ('music'), it just means 'playing with tones', you see. And so, she continues.

She wants to tell me about the special connection this church has with the Faroese language. It was in this warm, colorful church that the first ever sermon was given in Faroese in 1911. At the time, it was illegal to preach in any language other than Danish. Denmark had suppressed the Faroese language. It was seen as a deficient dialect, not fit for certain purposes. The Danes wanted the language of the Faroes to be Danish. But eight hundred miles away on a remote Faroese island, the tiny population of Sandvík had supported a pugilistic priest who was brave enough to break ranks.

These churches have an alluring simplicity. From the ceiling, brass candle chandeliers hang suspended next to model boats. The wooden pews are painted white with blue colonial ends: the colors of the ocean. Some of the church bells come from retired ships. There is a feeling of intimacy and localness here. This particular church was built in Froðba (a small settlement on the outskirts of Tvøroyri) and moved to Tvøroyri, both of which are on the island of Suðuroy. It had to be dismantled, put on a ship and then rebuilt in Sandvík in 1908 because Tvøroyri got its own church. These stories are common in the Faroes: mid-nineteenth century churches were carried bit-by-bit over mountains. What is more, a local poet, Paul F., wrote about the extraordinary life of the nineteenth century pall-bearers: tired, sodden men who carried coffins over mountains in mid-winter to the nearest church for burial. I loved these stories of stoic faith and hardship. They defined the Faroes, and I would hear such accounts everywhere I went.

After the service in Sandvík, a huddle of shy men stand in the antechapel. They whisper soft, looping narratives filled with cobwebs of nicknames. An awkward silence. Skewed, furtive glances. The church-goers are keen to know who the visitor is, but do not wish to put me on the spot. 'Where is he from in Norway?', I hear the local keeper of lost words mutter in Faroese. Once the ambiguities have been solved, the priest and a handful of worshippers step outside to smoke. And then under the blue fug of cigarette smoke, their words having spaced themselves into silence, they slowly disperse in the light drizzle. Even when it rains, there is a moody beauty here.

Blade Shears

Shearing sheep in the Faroe Islands

IN JULY WHEN THE weather is clear, the remaining sheep now dotted along the skyline, are rounded up from the slopes of the outfield (*hagar*). The outfield is the land outside the village that is partitioned into narrow strips. The Faroese have been grazing sheep in the summer on the outfields for about nine hundred years when the use of shielings (a hut used to pasture animals) was phased out. The *hagar* were also used previously for cutting peat and catching birds. Land in the Faroes is divided up using an ancient practice. The land of each village is allotted a set number of *merkur, gyllin* and *skinn,* the latter two being smaller denominations of the first. We are working Gudmund's land today; he has two *merkur* and three *gyllin* or thirty-five *gyllin* in total. The number of sheep you can farm on a *mørk* (singular of *merkur*) varies for the areal size of a *mørk* differs from village to village. Here you can have three sheep per *gyllin* or forty-eight per *mørk*. That means we have just over a hundred sheep to shear. Furthermore, the land is classified into *ognarjørð* (land inherited from previous generations) and *kongsjørð,* land which the Crown owns and initially gave as lease-holdings to Danish priests and nobles. There is still some status attached to farmers that farm *kongsjørð*. There was one of them in my valley.

Sheep have been the backbone of this society since the time of the Viking settlement a thousand years ago: the first Faroese constitution (*Seyðabrævið* 'Sheep Letter') in 1298 was a letter about sheep-breeding, the Faroe Isles means the 'Isles of Sheep' and the extremely hardy Faroese sheep has always been one of their main sources of food. Sheep management on the Faroes has remained more or less unchanged for centuries. The meat is used by the farmers themselves, and thus words such as 'productivity' have little meaning. There are no approved slaughter houses in the Faroes, so the farmers do it themselves. There are no official requirements for the registration of sheep, so the farmers keep count and commit it to memory. If there are disputes between neighboring farmers, they look back to their forebears and the 'Sheep Letter' from 1298 is consulted. Common grazing rights have meant sheep, land-ownership and farming families have been intertwined for as long as people can remember. Sheep outnumber people on the Faroes; approximately seventy thousand of these animals with so few flocking instincts roam the steep semi-scrubland. In spring, the sound of lambs bleating to their mothers echoes right through the valleys. Sometimes I would sit in the infield by the house, listen to that joyous sound and just let the world roll past me.

The organization of the round-up is today a little haphazard and disorderly. After what seemed like weeks of speculation as to which day it would happen, a flurry of quick phone-calls resulted in a rapidly agreed consensus that today was the day. The weather is fine and everybody is available. And so, we are now out on the fell, the unfenced common land. At this time of the year, the sheep are high up in the rough terrain of the mountain ridges. A skirl of shepherds and their helpers are driving the sheep carefully out of the crags and down through a cobweb of fences to a pen in front of the sheep house. Those who do not have a sheep house are using a make-shift pen in the middle of one of the tracks. Locals are shouting, whistling and waving their arms around. The fell-scented stock is rounded up twice a year, once in July for the *royting* ('sheep shearing') and once in September for the *skurð* ('slaughter'). It is now time for the *royting*. This will be the first time the farmers have seen their sheep for many weeks. At this time of the year, the sheep graze free from supervision on the fell-tops where the sky meets the land.

Here in Tvøroyri on the southernmost island of the Faroese archipelago, extended family and friends work together with a sheepdog to round up the sheep. Gathering is ancient communal work and today it's the new generation of farmers' first round-up. They will learn the rudiments of the *royting*. It is a little chaotic for our half-trained sheepdog is flanking but not maintaining a constant distance from the stock. The ewes with young lambs become frightened and aggressive when the dog gets too close to them. The owner tries to slow the dog down with a series of orders. After some confusion, the flock begins to surge down the mint-green slope. A small group of men and women walk down from the gaunt shoulders of the hills making sure that all the sheep are in front of them. The sheep are made up of scores of different color combinations, each with its own name. Eventually, the fractured fellowship forms more or less one flock, one unison bleat, and spaced out in a semi-circle behind them, the helpers guide them down through the infields to the pen. The ground is boggy and sodden, sucking them in with a soft belching sound. Rubber-wellied and resting on wooden hiking staves at the bottom of the slope, the elder statesmen if you like, observe the goings-on with knowing grins. A look of satisfaction invades their faces. The land has seeped into these men and you can see how their bloodlines flow through the ancestral pens. Families of farmers; flocks of sheep. One chalky-haired farmer carries a transistor radio in his pocket. He holds it occasionally to his ear to check the football score. The radio voice is excitable, hopping from crescendo to diminuendo. He nods, clears his throat and repeats above the din the score for the shearers who are sharpening their blades in anticipation. Across these islands, radios would be blaring and hearts swelling and thundering around kitchen tables adorned with cakes. Then, there is the sharp click of the iron gate-hook, and the sheep – the color of chess pieces – are knitted into the pen.

As the lambs are separated from their mothers, the air thickens with despair. An incessant orchestra of bleats between ewe and tup ensues and continues throughout the afternoon; the noise draws onlookers, jokers and sturdy women with Persian blue eyes and spiraling hair who lean against the railings. Islanders always stop to watch such events, even if they are totally familiar. Everybody is in high spirits as the shearers recycle jokes which are barely audible amidst the clamor. For these islanders, the *royting* represents the grandeur of island rural life. The lambs are herded off into the sheep shed where swallows explode outward from the door. These bundles of soft wool turn in tight concentric circles forming cogs of uncertainty that are constantly reconfigured as they become increasingly anxious. The shearing will last several hours. *Feðgar* ('fathers and sons') work in tandem, using just occasional words of instruction and shear a sheep with remarkable dexterity; a sheep is shorn in a flurry of darting, energetic flashes. Heavy, double-coated fleeces are tossed aside. Once the sheep are shorn, the lambs will have their ears clipped in accordance with a complex schema comprising fifty-four different *seðyamark* ('ear mark').

In the pen, Gudmund slides around in the sheep excrement, producing serial expletives. He grabs a ram by the horns and wrestles with it in the filth, before dragging it round to the shearing area. It takes two shearers to hold a ram down on a metal stand where he will be shorn. The head rests on a U-shaped piece of metal as if it were a guillotine, and then a bolt secures the head in place. Elbows spread on the railings, the onlookers nod. The sheep kick and struggle initially, but then relax once they know they are only being shorn. The wool is extremely thick and must be cut using blade shears:

'No machines here', shouts Stein, a chatty resident of Hvalba and employee of Gudmund.

'They leave the animal with no wool. No good for our climate'. To start the shearing, you cut the wool right at the back end of the sheep, running the blade up the sheep's back', instructs Gudmund.

The air is full of the smells of decomposing sebum; the wool smells warm. I stand with nostrils open. The inner wool is yellowy, greasy with lanolin or wool wax. The women rub the lanolin into their hands, suggesting I do likewise. I am told it protects both the sheep's and human's skin from the environment:

'pooh...ha...it is hard work', says Gudmund in his hoarse voice.

My jeans are blotched with sheep-shit. It seems to have taken me an eternity to shear my first sheep and the ram does not look too pleased with my efforts:

'Aha, *tu erst Føroyingar nå*...yes, you are Faroese' laughs Stein.

We take a break. Excited words pass between us. Súsanna, Gudmund's wife, serves black coffee and homemade chocolate cake. The women speak of recent memories of shearing. Last year, it was a battle to get it done before the rain started. Súsanna looks over to the sheep-shed and says 'but I think this year, we are in luck'. Thirty or so ewes stir anxiously on the other side of the pen. Skittish, they turn in sharp circles, bawling. Ásbjørn, an elderly farmer from Tvøroyri, sits on a stool, the ear marking pliers in hand, and punches holes in the lamb's ears as if he were a train ticket inspector. Each farm has its own earmark symbol. Ours is *bragd frammanundan* which looks something like a 'V' shaped clip on the left-hand side of the ear.

Drops of blood stain the soft, springy wool. The lambs leave the fold slightly traumatized, hopping over invisible fences. A little unsteady on their feet, the released prisoners are then reunited with their anxious mothers, and the flow out onto the fell recommences. I keep tally: fifty-one lambs, twenty-six ewes, twenty-five rams. My tally marks are clustered in groups of five matchstick men with the fifth man held diagonally by the four upstanding soldiers. The whole extended family comes together to pile up the wool in the sheep shed. It will be cleaned and sorted, although nobody is sure what to do with wool these days. It has not been a cash crop for about eighty years. The scent of burning wool from a neighboring fold already lingers in the infields leaves a clue. The groups of *feðgar*, smelling of lanolin, shit and rain retire towards Gudmund's house. Gudmund is a strong believer in eating after communal work and callousing labor. There in the evening, we all dine on blood pancakes and potatoes under a vicious sunset. It has been a long day and the older men stifle yawns, look furtively at their wrists and start to drift off beneath ruddy skies and thickening shadows. It is gone eleven o'clock.

Winter Visitors
Mainland exiles

IN THE BRIEF SUMMER months, hardy sheep graze on lime-colored turf-roofed homes amidst the shrill *peep-ing* calls of the oystercatcher. Obstreperous starlings trapeze and spar on the twisted steel of barbed wire fences. All year round, skittish sheep with few flocking instincts defend territorially the verges of tracks and minor roads from slow passing motor vehicles. Reluctant to disperse, their infectious bleats echo in the stiff, wintry air. The sheep here are tame and will eat out of your hand.

As we move north, puffy cauliflower clouds march briskly across the horizon. We pass through fickle, ephemeral weather systems. One moment the islands are lost in northern mist and drizzle, and the next sparkle in the prismatic colors of the late afternoon rainbow. All that was just yesterday faded green, is now white. The soft, diffused light of early November is vague and uncertain; the sky a spectrum of various shades of grey and ivory.

Beyond Klaksvík, tiered basalt and red tuff, volcanic in shape, rise sharply from the sea, up to several hundred meters. The lower half, greenish-grey of lichen covered rock, the upper half, antique white with a thin layer of snow. Sometimes, topped in arêtes and tarns. The narrow road winds us round inky, crinkled fjords, stony crags and eroding cliffs in a dim light. Sometimes, right up to the cliff edge.

We, mainland exiles, pass clusters of symmetrical houses painted in primary colors, each distinguished from the other through the window-frame color scheme. Splashes of green, red and yellow: each with its own view onto the howling Atlantic. Houses that sit by the sea, gathered around a wooden church, hugging the end of narrow fjords, at the bottom of steep valleys sheltered from the wind. There might be nobody there, but all the homes sit on the kinship circuit. Small pious communities built around spatially distinctive *bygdir* ('villages or settlements'), summoned to church on windy days.

On the island of Borðoy, we drive through a series of one lane, un-lit tunnels with damp, dripping rock. Intriguing Kafkaesque death-traps bored in the 1960s and 70s by taciturn engineers. Out of the darkness, back to the meandering, littoral road and through protected snowy sounds to Hvannasund. The normal, private hush after snowfall. Then, waiting for the ferry, two passers-by ask us with a shy curiosity where we are going. The answer is followed by a nodding of heads and a *ja,ja, nettup* 'yes, yes, indeed'. There is some doubt as to whether the ferry will leave in the bad weather. *Kanska* 'perhaps'. Nobody can know for sure.

* * *

Fugloy, the most inaccessible of the northern Faroese archipelago, does not tend to receive visitors in mid-winter. Aboard the *Ritan*, a retired trawler, we are the only passengers. The *Merkið* flutters in the impatient breeze. There is a captain and a drunken shipmate who reeks of methylated spir-its and staggers around the deck amidst the stinging sea-spray. He is from Svínoy. From cliff to cliff, the ferry chugs between the *oyjggar* ('islands'), plying its route between the partially hidden, jagged promontories of the Atlantic towards the bluff headland. The sea becomes agitated, an easterly wind scythes across the open water; *Ritan* pitches and sways in the swirl and stomachs begin to churn. We pass Svínoy where mist-hewn houses sink into the nebulous oblivion of the *pollamjørki*, ('low-lying fog with good weather above') and dank tracks are almost hidden in wisps of low brume. The shipmate regales stories in an incoherent slur about the worst winter storms, the bonds formed at sea and his collateral relatives dotted around the northern islands. Approaching Fugloy, the final shafts of the day's sun-light appear through the gaps in the dark, battle-smoke-like clouds giving the island a subliminal glow.

* * *

We arrive in stormy mid-winter to the settlement of Hattarvík on the eastern side of the island where as a rule the shores slope into the sea. Hattarvík has a winter population of just three; a former Viking settlement with evidence of ancient farming and the alleged home of a group of Faroese separatists, the so-called *Flokksmenn*. Today, the last all-year-round inhabitants live in a village of abandoned houses amidst turf-roofed *hjallur* ('drying sheds ventilated by the wind'), with hanging *skerpikjøt* ('wind-dried mutton') and redundant *neyst* ('boathouse') which house a farrago of rudders, oars and nautical miscellany.

There is no mooring, no jetty or quay. The boat heaves up and down violently in the rough water; the jump has to be timed perfectly to coincide with the top of the swell. A slight mistake and the dark, angry sea awaits. Two piebald border collies samba in the wind, anxious to escort the queasy arrivals. An elderly man greets us silently at the shore. Answers to questions are monosyllabic, if at all. A nodding valediction.

We walk up the narrow, steep path from the shore lit by the broad shoulders of streetlights whose noses point down inquisitively. Crunching under foot, we trudge through the heavy snow, past empty houses in silence. Spokes of an old, buckled wheel, jaundiced patches of urine and fritters of excrement decorate the virgin surface, tampering with its aesthetic of purity. A fresh carpet of snow extends beyond the *bygd*; a white, Irish linen tablecloth, starched and perfect, without the slightest knob or slub.

The wind has dropped. It is calm; not a whisper. There is an orange wan stain on the horizon; the twilight of a faded postcard. Candles flicker in the few remaining houses that are inhabited. Private narratives sit behind netted curtains in the garnished living rooms of their caulked homes. Elderly men sit in the kitchen listening to the *andlát*, ('news of the dead') broadcast on the radio twice a day where the names of those Faroese that have died in recent days are read out in a low, sinister voice. A society of obituaries where surnames merge with place-names; the Fuglø of Fugloy.

A brawny figure stares at us with an expressionless face from slightly parted curtains, watching our every movement from elected isolation. The room is lit up by a silent television set; Test Card F in cyan, magenta and blue plays in the background. We speculate on when he last saw a winter visitor. During the winter months, there is even less talk. When nothing happens, there is nothing to say (*noi, ongin at siga*). A desire for isolation and simplicity becomes a personal battle. Romanticism in a wintry adagio; a reclusive chore on tired evenings that rest on stubs of time.

Our house is painted white and green with racing green window frames. Lots of small rooms serve specific functions. It has that timeless appeal found in Faroese and Icelandic houses in the countryside. An anomaly in the world of time; it has a cinematic appeal. There is a small rectangular kitchen table by the window with a colorful red vinyl tablecloth with yellow spots. A pair of heavy 1980s binoculars on the window ledge. An ageing Hi-Fi unit; the radio is to be heard everywhere across the islands: in public saunas, public toilets, offices, garages, workshops, aboard ships etc. I turn the chrome knob: ring-dancing from Sumba. The voice of the *skipari* ('leader'), the onomatopoeic words and the steady, hypnotic rhythm of the dance and stamping feet that goes around and around in dizzying semi-circles. Hand-in-hand, tight, meandering loops of Faroese dancers – men and women, boys and girls – symbolize the intertwined social order of Faroese society.

My room, up through the trap door and to the left, a small, overheated oubliette, looks out onto the *seyðahus* ('sheep outhouse'). There are a few musty Faroese books on the shelf. The pages are discolored, brittle with foxed, tan stains: a story of a Faroese missionary's stay in Guyana; a 1946 edition of the *Nýggja Testamenti*. I thumb through the stiff pages and soon fall asleep to the light of the waxing gibbous trickling through the window.

I awake to the sound of the clapper striking the swinging, cast bronze church bell in a *ritardando* tempo. The red-roofed church is a shelter from the screeching wind. Like an ill-formed testudo, the *hattarvíkingar* shield themselves from the driving sleet, and shuffle past the yawning church doors. The wood panel walls are painted white, the pews blue; the colors of the surf and the ocean. The Lutheran service is simple and by the book: a cross-stitch of litany, hymns and readings. Candles are lit. The lay-preacher, parish clerk and bell-ringer reads slowly and carefully from the Book of Matthew. A metallic voice rasps tinnily. The tiny congregation has time aplenty to dwell on the meaning of the words, suspended in the cool air. A mêlée of *dj-dj* fricatives, reminiscent of squelching mud on a soggy heath, but the apotheosis of lyrical expression. A language whose bending vowels and elongated diphthongs give it a candid, rural feel.

Year after year, the numbers attending the Church went down as people left Hattarvík. Fifteen years ago, there were just six men and one woman living here in the winter. The lay-preacher has been in post since 1964, the other two church-goers, wearing patterned *troyggjur* ('woolen sweaters') and enigmatic stares, sit in their normal places; well apart from one another, towards the back, in adjacent aisles in the simple wooden church. They peer out through the narrow Gothic windows onto the sea, pondering the cargos of memories past.

The last inhabitants are alone with nature and their nostalgic thoughts here. And, that is all. But, it is not bleak. It is just another rural elegy of sheep-farmers and crofters, and is life on this rocky periphery, this crumbling edge. It is said that loneliness is killing the place. Some believe that soon there will be just summer houses, the briny tang, the billing gannets on the cliff edge of the *gjógv* ('gorge'), the endless onslaught of the sea. The memories will live on. In times of adversity, *deus ex machina*-less tragedies have played out here. Boys swept off the rocky shore and into the exploding, unforgiving maelstrom whilst hymns are sung to a swirling wind. A precarious life; man small as a homunculus again in the face of nature.

The drama of living on a remote Atlantic outpost in the absolute worst of the Faroese weather is a five-act play with the *dénouement* only in May. During the winter months on the northern Faroese coast, Hattarvík is smashed by one angry storm after another; the swell that crashes against the cliffs is deafening, roaring and rumbling. The tiny settlement disappears rhythmically behind a wall of raging white foam.

A dying village, a metaphor for rural decline perhaps; the feel of sorrow shambles down from terraced outfield to the crumbling shore. A *bygd* that is almost decommissioned, like the local lighthouse.

And so Hattarvík is alive with a jumble of memories, curdled dreams and spirits. The stones still speak. A dozen houses gathered around a rocky bay, looking boldly out to sea, a spacious church, a plethora of rickety *hjallur*, a burnt down school point to former times. The last residents sit and wait for *Másin*, the daily post boat, a merciful routine, or perhaps for the telephone to ring. Amidst the chads of a forgotten existence, they sit and wait for a way of life to come to an end; like that of the lighthouse keeper. There is little to do here, but to listen to the keening noise of the wind and speculate on the uncertain future that beetles over the place. If the weather is good, you might go to the sheepfold.

* * *

Calligraphic lanes wind up precipitously through the white escarpment, past forgotten shielings, drunk, wattled fences and towards Kirkja, the other *bygd* on the island with a population of ten. The lethargic winter sun rises behind us, inching towards its December solstice. The cairned path takes us up two hundred meters, across buckled land and past summer breeding grounds for coalitions of sea birds. Shrieking gulls that squabble and bicker like parliamentarians for weeks on end.

Sleeping Hattarvík sits behind us, nestled securely in the bay, whist and unruffled. The track bends to the right and then drops sharply. Scattered, rusting farm machinery, skid steers and mulching heads, peak through the fresh snow. Unforgiving mountain ridges with peaks plummeting perpendicularly to the sea mark the north coast of Viðoy.

A solitary Faroese horse with a heavy winter coat and ambling gait comes towards us. One of the rarest breeds in the world, he is especially photogenic: the color of the small patches of exposed basalt adjacent to us, moving on a white sheet of snow marked only by his warm, lonely footprints; the entire image is black-and-white and gives a pleasing calmness. With raised, dilated nostrils, he snorts at the unexpected walkers. Peaceful breath; a face full of nobility.

We approach Kirkja, named after a medieval church that once stood here. The path zig-zags through the rock, down to the larger, but relatively emptier island *bygd*. The majority of the remaining residents are at a local wedding on Svínoy; a Fugloy lad married a Svínoy girl, giving some hope for the islanders of the North.

Kirkja is set up on the hill, away from the sea which is reached by a snaking, railed path. There are empty houses with tired clocks and piles of tatty, black and white photographs sprawled out over dusty tables; eddies of memories swirling in the incorrigible wind on afternoons slick with rain. The never-ending rain that sings a morning madrigal, running down the gutters of Kirkja's steep lanes and the puddled pavements glazed in the light of the nostalgic latticed church windows. Vagrant sheep and dogs register our presence, but there appear to be no people.

There is little time; the Sámal Joensen-Mikines church altar painting of Christ walking on water will have to be foregone. The *Ritan* is on its way from Svínoy. Her Oxford blue hull bounces along the choppy water. The boat cannot moor; the shipmate yells to us to jump aboard as soon as she arrives.

The faded yellow houses of Kirkja glow in the distance in the soft, mysterious winter morning light with its soothing bluish tones. Over towards Borðoy, there is a sallow gleam; a few strands of wispy, feathery cirrus cloud paint the sky, hanging sublimely over the rounded isthmus of Viðareiði. We are on our way to Svínoy where peat used to be cut and Vikings are buried. The intention is to pick up some of the heavy-headed wedding guests, but for the moment we are the only passengers. *Ritan* bobs like a cork across the open water; the view from the spray covered portholes is quickly washed away. Cargo begins to slide; the gimlet-eyed shipmate who has joined us in the lower-deck to punch our tickets grins and smiles at the oddity of the winter visitors.

Hoyggja
Harvesting grass in the Faroe Islands

JULY IS THE TIME of the *hoyggja* which refers to the cutting of the in-field
(*bøur*) grass and harvesting it for the sheep's winter feed. Families are outside; their cheery voices drift in the wind. Children's laughter sweeps across
the fields. There is noise everywhere. Flies hum heavily. I hear the haunting
curlews, the ghosts of dead boys, on the horizon. The air tremors with their
distinctive call. High up on the mountain ridges, skuas defend the spines
of the hills. A woman's brassy voice can be heard jabbering from a nearby
window, her sentences shrinked to disconnected words. There is the sound
of scythes being whetted. Radios are perched on the stumps of fence posts.
Their aerials waltzing in the wind. Music plays. Dogs bark.

Leaning on two-tined pitch-forks, elderly men with creased brows
stand around exchanging gossip. Their voices dangle in the light breeze.
The farmers nod as they listen to an account of a wet harvest two score
years ago. They square their shoulders and lower their tones as the lay-
reader shuffles by, his shoes grinding on the gravel. Then the conversation
turns to lawnmower designs. They all swear by a certain liver-shaped Italian brand that is used to negotiate the very uneven ground of the steep
slopes. But first the long, tickling grass has to be scythed. With scythe
in hand, I cast a glance over the hills and see elderly men scything with
obstreperous grandchildren at their feet collecting the grass. This rural
scene, this summer idyll could be from a hundred years ago. Further up
the bank where Gudmund and his extended family are at work, Stein from
Hvalba talks endlessly about the *huldufólk* ('supernatural, elf-like spirits
to be found in the Faroese countryside') of Lítla Dímun (the uninhabited
island without electricity where sheep are taken to graze in a smack). His

conversation turns to the intertwining of the visible and the invisible, the material and the spiritual. The places where the stones speak to the ocean. Families battled over ownership of Lítla Dímun, this tiny nipple of basalt in the mid-Atlantic, for many years. In the end, a cooperative of forty-eight farmers from Hvalba bought the island and still keep their sheep on this mysterious, unsettled outpost. The talk switches to politics, parliamentary squabbles, fishing quotas and the dead. Telling stories seems to be an essential part of *hoyggja*. It is a time to meet with friends, laugh, pass on memories from previous harvests and of course prepare the grass. Then, orders wrapped in a shower of expletives are barked at Stein and it is back to work. The people of Suðuroy (the southernmost island that makes up the archipelago) are known for their expressiveness, their sometimes crass language, operatic nerves and the way they wave their arms around when they speak.

It is a dry summer's day and we are busy raking the grass and placing it on long drying racks (*turkilagar*) that line the hilly pastures running from top to bottom. Flocks of starlings feast noisily on clews of worms that are revealed as the rake drags across the earth. Covered in nets, the grass is left to dry on these racks in the wind. It is imperative that the grass is dried as much as possible before the rain comes which can be taxing in the Faroes. More than the rain, the farmers fear fog and windless days. Providing there is wind, the grass normally dries even if there is the odd shower of rain. This summer has been rather dry and the farmers are hopeful that we will have a good harvest of hay to feed the sheep over the winter. Sunshine has been forecast for the whole week and all going well the grass should be sun-bleached in ten days or so. If the grass gets very wet, it turns into a soggy mush, a useless liability and a rotting curse. Nowadays, it is less important than it was before. Almost no farmers are dependent on just sheep anymore and some now have silos to make silage. Previously, a wet harvest could have had disastrous consequences. This is the last day of harvesting the grass to make silage. Everyone is helping out to make sure the job is done. Aside from the grass that is being dried the old-fashioned way, this grass will be stored in airtight silos and fermented using formic acid and water. Men tread the grass in silos as if it were grapes; they try to squeeze out as much of the air as possible. There is little baling here for the ground is so uneven and the slopes are so steep. That must in part explain why farming methods are barely unchanged.

After a long, hard day in the fields, we are fed *ræst kjøt* at Gudmund's house. *Ræst kjøt* is lamb that has been air-dried for several months and then braised for seven hours. With few trees and no salt production due to adverse weather conditions, the Faroese were not able to smoke or salt meat to preserve it. The pungent smell of *ræst kjøt*, somewhere between a veiny cheese, lamb and wool hits you as you enter the kitchen. The meat is served with root vegetables. The meat comes from the sheep that were slaughtered in September. Gudmund sells the meat privately to local people and distributes the rest to his extended family. Almost all the meat is eaten air-dried. The Faroese love to eat their food prepared in this fashion.

Dinner finished, we stand outside on the veranda. Laconic speech comes from the adjacent living room. The air is crisp and fresh. Tonight, it tastes of the sea. The view over the green slopes and the principalities of sheep that border the fjord could only be the Faroes. The gullied hills, the vestiges of a glacial age, that wrinkle the bare rock. Houses, painted the colors of the rainbow, hug the bay. As is often the case this time of the year, the fuchsia-colored sunset has invaded the sky by the rounded peaks that cradle the fjord. The Trongisvágur valley looks like a Mikines oil painting with the evening glow gushing across the horizon. Gudmund clears his throat and tells me repeatedly how he loves this view. The Faroese take great pride in their country. Elderly women in the village would often be seen photographing every detail of the local landscape even if they had spent their entire life there. They never tire of its beauty even if everything is strikingly familiar. Late in the evening, we retire under the scattered light of the fading sun to homes warmed by the summer sunshine and to kitchens alive with radio noise.

Drying grass in the Faroes

The Scent of Angelica

Traveling the ancestral paths in the Faroe Islands

THE DAY BEGINS ON the quay at Tvøroyri on the southernmost island of the Faroes. Held by their horns, rams are loaded into the make-shift wooden pen that occupies the stern of a fishing vessel. This dozen or so rams belong to part-time farmers in Tvøroyri, and they are on their way to Hvannhaga (*hagi* being the 'summer grazing land'), a lush spot on the east of the island where angelica grows. Angelica, a plant native to the sub-Arctic region, was the main source of Vitamin C for the Faroese in the past. A small number of selected rams are taken to Hvannhaga in May of each year, and collected again in September when the farmers slaughter them in the basements of their own houses. Grazing over the short summer on remote cliff edges, their meat is said to have an entirely different taste. To get them to their new pastures, the sheep have to be hitched in plastic bags up the vertical cliff faces that hem the shore. Nowadays, such a practice of transporting sheep to the most inaccessible spots on the islands is part animal husbandry, part cultural tradition and part sport. It is a tradition that the Faroese have maintained for centuries and is a time for a cooperative of smallholders to come together, travel the ancestral paths and sail the channels of their forebears. It is one of the ways by which the Faroese seek security in the memory where they come from.

Waiting at the dock, there soon assembles a welter of elderly men dressed in patterned sweaters and short wellies who have come to observe the goings-on. Everything quickly becomes a group effort. The work involving sheep, especially the *royting* or 'gathering of the wool', is shared. It is a time for community, an opportunity to show the next generation how to work the land. On board the vessel, *Sjóriddarin*, congregate a dozen men of very different ages, but of related countenance. They each own one or two rams on the boat, each sheep has a name but is referred to by its colors and markings: *framgráur* ('grey front'), *fóthvitur* ('white foot') *morreyður* ('reddish brown') etc. One of these steely-eyed men from neighboring Hvalba grabs my hand, saying:

'Welcome. Einar. I work in offshore drilling, six weeks on, six weeks off. We Faroese cannot live from sheep', he adds.

Although the morose characters of Danish detective thrillers that fill our television screens may be clad in Faroese jumpers, there is no money in sheep wool these days:

'No longer *færøysk gull* 'Faroese gold'', he shouts above the sputtering engine.

The knitwear companies do not even pay farmers in cash for the wool. They are paid in jumpers. These jumpers known as *troyggjar* pile up in their homes, overspilling from farmers' wardrobes:

'Yes, it is difficult to make a living from sheep', an older cousin of his continues. 'Sheep-farming is full of uncertainties. Sometimes when we have a *felli* ('a high mortality of sheep due to a harsh winter') we might lose a third of the flock'. No good', he says. 'No good'. 'Our future is in the sea now. Mackerel and herring'.

Aboard *Sjóriddarin*, we leave the safety of the Tvøroyri harbor and I grin at the prospect of the unknown adventure that beckons. The boat bobs up and down and the dots of light in the distance begin to wobble and shake. Through a splintered window, I spot tube-nosed fulmars, once oil for the islanders' lamps and the staple food for the people living on the now abandoned Scottish island of St Kilda. With stiff wings, these birds undulate in time with the turf-colored sea. Some Faroese still eat fulmars, and speak of the foul-smelling oil that they spit at intruders to their nests on the cliffs. *Fúllmár* in Old Norse meant literally the 'foul smelling gull'. I think of the gritty men who dined more regularly on such catch and who amongst coiled ropes and wave-washed gulls worked on diesel-scented boats such as this. Their faces and idioms were surely shaped by the wind, sunken homilies and the infinities of the sea. Some of them were washed up on rocky outposts such as Stóra Dímun where "sons died in the fast currents".

Stóra Dímun lies just north-east of Suðuroy, the island where Tvøroyri is located. Before us, it rises several hundred meters out of the sea in Celtic isolation (Dímun is almost certainly a Celtic name). At the top of this barely habitable rock measuring just one square mile and in the shape of a squashed hexagon lives a family of four amongst tens of thousands of storm petrels and puffins. They manage a wind-swept farm, nestled behind a two-meter-thick stone wind-breaker and anchored down with steel ropes. Without these reinforcements, the farmhouse would be totally exposed and ripped to pieces in the storms. With a lighthouse for company, the farm clings to the austere and implacable shadows of the unfeasibly green escarpment. The family is alone here; alone with the echoes of the past and the radio voice on those soot-black nights of winter. Fertilized by the guano of millions of birds that have for thousands of years made it their home, the soil offers excellent grazing for several hundred ewes. But, sheep farming on Stóra Dímun comes with an unusual set of challenges. Farmers and visiting ministers have been blown off the island to quick deaths. It used to be the case that a Lutheran minister had to visit the island twice a year to hold a service in the church that once stood there. In 1874, the visiting minister of Sandoy fell from the rocks whilst climbing up from the landing stage and died. I had overheard many such stories whilst traveling back and forth to Tórshavn.

Beneath scribbles of cloud, our boat follows the coastline round to the east, past Froðba, a mysterious cave and headland named by Scottish sailors. Kittiwakes pursue us effortlessly on either side of the boat whilst guillemots and puffins skim the edge of the water. Ahead, on the outskirts of Froðba, an orange windsock marking the helipad blows in the whirring wind. On deck, men dressed in knitwear saw off the pointed ends of their *sárningur*'s curling horns. A *sárningur* is a ram whose long horns have grown very close to the face. My gaze shifts from the sheep to the cliff tops where they are headed. All along the coastline, sheep graze implausibly on sixty-degree cliff edges that appear almost vertical from the vantage point of the prow-shaped deck. I am relieved to hear from my companions that the sheep seldom lose their footing and drop into the sea that lies a couple of hundred meters beneath them.

I join the skipper in the cabin of the boat. He speaks in an archaic local dialect cutting off the ends of words and gluing them together. He revives metaphors in a slow, raspy voice:

'Yes, the dialects are fascinating. But they disappear slowly', he shouts above the engine noise. 'Almost there now', he says with renewed concentration.

He aims the boat for a slope by the cliff edge, stained white with guano, and lying just behind a peaked islet with mythical shaped edges. From the cliff summit, two bemused sheep stare down at the trespassers. Fifty meters or so from the rocky shore, Gudmund who organized today's outing, loosens the cleat hitch and hops into the aluminum rowing boat that we have been towing. The tidal current is strong, and with five passengers he rows with all his might to the shore. He gestures to the sky and the barely visible moon which is almost full:

'Fast current. It is the moon', he laughs. I watch the excitement scatter across his face.

Gudmund's family have been the pillar of Tvøroyri society for generations. They were ship-owners, landowners and men of letters. He is a kind man, always willing to help and contribute. He likes to bring people together and do what he can for the community. Gudmund talks endlessly of the small-minded politics and jealousy that characterize the more remote, outer settlements. Somehow, he manages to rise above it all, even the arguments created by the arcane land-ownership laws that can leave busy village halls awash with sunken glances on chalky faces as information is whispered nervously from ear to ear. Known for his coruscating wit and shunning the theology of personal success, Gudmund subscribes instead to 'the religion of kindness'. I remember meeting Gudmund in the silhouettes of early summer after one of the rowing regattas. He dropped everything to show a stranger every crook and cranny of this island that his family has called home for centuries.

Five sprightly men well into their sixties hop out of the dinghy that Gudmund is rowing and start to climb deftly up the slippery rocks to secure the rope at the top of the cliff edge fifty meters or so above them. It seems to be just a matter of minutes before the men reach the top. Judging by the way they scale the rocks, it is obvious that these Faroese are at home on these shores defined by their arches and sea-stacks. Then, onboard our boat, anxious rams whose rectangular pupils scan the cliffs for fellow members of the flock, are turned upside down, their legs are roped together and they are lowered into the rowing boat bobbing around on the swirl. Ferried to the shore, the manacled sheep are each placed like hostages into a sturdy bag and then these heavy parcels are hitched up the rocks by those waiting at the top. The tugging of the rope is perfectly synchronized, and the sheep are granted a relatively smooth passage up the rock face. Prized out of their bags, and unshackled, the sheep soon clamber up the vertiginous, knife-like edge of the cliff and start grazing. Grass is grass.

The job is soon done and the doughty climbers pile into the tiny cabin to joke with the skipper and share Faroese food. They warm themselves with black coffee from the Thermos, some of it slopping on the floor in the swirl. The skipper with his undefeated eyes sermonizes the virtues of enacting such old traditions:

'We have always done it this way', he says. 'I remember as a boy watching my grandfather climb the cliffs'. We might be no longer farmers, but part of us still belongs to the old ways of doing things, you know', he continues.

There is much agreement and mutual back-patting. These men, each bearing a nickname, take small slices of bread, spread goose fat on the bread and then cut a thin piece from the leg of *skerpikjøt* which we have brought with us. This shank of wind-dried mutton has the color and texture of venison, and smells pungent. As is tradition, it has been hanging in Gudmund's drying shed for eight months:

'The secret to good *skerpikjøt* is to kill the sheep early, at the beginning of September', he says with a gleeful face, before looking around and laughing '*ja, ja*, but not everybody agrees with me...'.

The Faroese love their food to taste of nature, and lamb and fish is often left to dry in the wind. It is home-slaughtered and home-prepared. But preparing *skerpikjøt* is an intricate art form governed by day and night air temperatures, the wind, salt content in the air, position of *hjallur* ('a drying-shed ventilated by the wind'), type of wood the *hjallur* is made of, how close the wooden panels are to one another, when the meat was hung, how the weather was after the first week it was hung etc. Knowledge of sheep and food preparation is refined and encyclopedic, but there is seldom consensus. It is generally agreed for instance that lamb or mutton from the west coast of Kalsoy which is a long, narrow island in the northern part of the archipelago, tastes better than the meat from the east coast. It is thought the west coast of this island gets slightly more sunshine. But, if you want to eat tallow, a hard fatty substance made from rendered mutton fat, and the Faroese do, it is said that it is best to pasture your sheep on the east coast (in the northern islands). I ask Gudmund why:

'I am not sure. It is just that way', he says shrugging his shoulders.

Whilst some of the men chew on *skerpikjøt*, a few others smoke roll-up cigarettes. The cigarettes hang precariously from the corners of their mouths. The silver-haired men grin and start to air concepts of justice. They like to interrogate the world. Talk turns to fishing politics as they start to spread the kidney-shaped cod roe from Gudmund's cousin on their bread:

'There are too many chiefs, and not enough Indians', offers Gudmund. *Ja, ja*. Mutual nodding. 'Fish is all we have, you know' [...] 'The cod and the halibut…They have been overfished. It is not good' offers Peter, a close friend of Gudmund whose sunken eyes are almost hidden below a great surge of eyebrow.

After a thought-brewing silence, the conversation moves on to the intricacies of boat-building; a skill that seems to be in their blood. The traditional clinker-built Faroese rowing boats are tar-coated and have that distinctive Viking shape, shallow hulled and made for rough seas with long, slender blades. These wooden boats pummel against the waves in all weathers. They seat eight people coated in sea spray and sweat, two by two by two by two on four planks of wood. At the Ólavsøka (the national holiday), traditionally dressed men and women, bards and preachers, fishermen and shepherds scramble down to the shore for the best view of the races. The competition between the villages is fierce and shaped by moderate jealousy:

'We build the boats just as our ancestors did, you know. The art has not been forgotten', says Peter contentedly with one eye on the sea.

The remaining men hover around the cabin and they agree that we should start to head back. On our way back to Tvøroyri, we stop off to explore a nearby sea cave of shadows where ringed seal are to be found in September. The cave is perhaps thirty meters deep, a damp, dripping chamber full of folklore. And then, Gudmund decides that the two of us should walk back to Tvøroyri together over the mountain instead of taking the boat round the coast:

'It is a beautiful walk. You should see it', he says.

We head ashore in the rowing boat to negotiate our path up the spongy slopes and through a dream-like landscape of gorges, exposed hilltops and empty valleys that fill quickly with candy floss-like-cloud. Pausing for breath, we watch as cloud sweeps in, enveloping us in seconds. The temperature plummets. Some minutes later, the clouds are gone. That is how it is here.

We follow cairns, piles of rocks that mark a network of ancient paths across the islands once used by shepherds, postmen, traders and merchants of meat, grain, wool and whale oil. These tracks trace narratives, relationships and historical events. The path rises sharply. Gudmund picks up the pace, telling stories in broken-breath about the *huldufólk* ('the hidden people'), the spirits or genius loci that live beneath the rocks. Here, the supernatural remains a possibility; the wondrous interplay between the seen and the unseen has not been lost. Listening to Gudmund, I scribble down a few words in my notebook. It is said that the 'hidden people' dislike electricity; they don't like it when the wires hum:

'There are *huldufólk* here. Oh, yes. That is for sure', says Gudmund.

The truncated conversation turns to *framsíggin* who are the people with special powers to see and hear *huldufólk*. It is said these people can also see others' futures. Gudmund thinks that many people dream of *huldufólk*, but few would admit to being a *framsíggin*:

'But, they exist', he insists. 'They exist'.

This network of paths marked out by cairns were put in place all over the Faroese archipelago to link the hundred or so villages. Nobody knows by whom or when. Our path meanders through the alternating dark and softer shelves of grass on the stepped cliffs rising to a few hundred meters. These shelves of grass on the slopes of the cliffs are called *hamrar*. The distinctive *hamrar* give the mountainsides a tiered appearance and are home to fulmars' nests. The crevices (*gjár*) in these stepped cliffs are particularly lush, full of woodrush, wild celery and wood cranesbill. On such *hamrar* and in a pale northern dusk, whimbrels can be heard calling to one another in a high-pitched frenzy. Behind me, the surface of Vatnið í Hvannhaga as the lake at Hvannhaga is known, is glassy and perfect. We stop. A nacreous sky skims overhead. Gudmund has heard something. He holds his index finger vertically to his lips:

'Listen, can you hear it?', whispers Gudmund.

From somewhere on the surface of the lake, the mournful haunting wail of the great northern diver beckons us back. We stop in a square of sunlight, mesmerized by the call of solitude. First the yodeling, and then the ghostly, transcendental echo of the wail that resonates through the valley as the bird seeks its mate. The sound nails you to the ground, tying sinew and soul together. We listen, waiting for the eerie, descending call that torpedoes the silence every thirty seconds or so. I could imagine these birds that live for decades calling to me in those drenched evenings conducive to introspection, calling me back again and again to this heavenly place.

The wail is broken by a spray of birds that appear from near the lake's edge. More and more appear and then what has become a thick cloud of birds bank and rise above us before plunging in looping, acrobatic formations. As unexpected as the call of the diver, this murmuration of starlings pulsates quite suddenly across the sky, contracting and expanding in the shape of a jellyfish. The sky becomes dark with birds as they make their preparations to roost. Moments of grace unfold before us as thousands of birds move in perfect unison fluidly across the sky. Sumptuous images, coiled in words, breed instantly. We sit amongst the musky, sacred scent of angelica to watch this bewitching and calming display of somersaults, twists and turns. I am ravished by the beauty of the world.

The birds eventually weave around the bay and disappear from sight. The sky is blank again. Gudmund and I share a smile and contented with this candescent memory we pick ourselves up from the moss cushion and move on up the hill. We pass disused *gróthús* ('stone sheds') where in olden times meat used to dry, and a damaged *hoyggjhús* ('hay shed') long devoid of hay. Gudmund talks of how in past years men have lost their lives abseiling down nearby cliffs to collect gulls' eggs to eat. There are just a few that do it now. The cairned path climbs further, leaving the mother-of-pearl cloudscape behind, and then we reach a plateau and look down into the Trongisvágsfjørður, as the fjord is called. The view is that of a promised land in a world of miniature: a place of bird calls, ridges, edges and corniches, where humans are fenced in by nature and not vice versa. Gudmund looks back, staring down into the empty valley and across the verdant knolls:

'The Google people have been here', he says. 'I don't like it'. 'I thought there might be somewhere free of satellite imagery', he sputters before walking on.

We descend into the valley through patches of cotton grass, cuckoo flower and marsh marigold and immediately come upon an oystercatcher mating dance: a military parade more or less as six tuxedoed birds march in tandem at great speeds with their flame-colored beaks pointing to the ground. Beneath the oystercatchers, small pick-up trucks pass by with attentive border collies as passengers, navigating the narrow, looping lanes which extend like tentacles from tiny villages. Vikings used to carry out heathen sacrifices in these villages. Tonight, there is a festival in one of them, Hov, and ring-dancers dressed as Vikings start to sing outside under a rising moon. All those long notes on unaccented syllables and short notes on accented syllables. Warmed by the fire, men and women of all ages look up to the sky, hand-in-hand and facing inwards, as they sing the words of the old, strongly syllabic Faroese ballads (*kvæðir*) which speak of lost kings and mythical battles. These ballads form an unbroken chain of learning as they were passed down orally from generation to generation for centuries. And the words of the better-known ballads are known by everybody. There is a localness to the ballads with different villages crafting their own version of the melody.

As we approach Tvøroyri and the quay where we started out from, we hear a screaming coxswain on the fjord, his traditional clinker-planked rowing boat darting impressively across the top of the water. They are preparing for the Ólavsøka regatta to be held next week in Tórshavn. We walk down the steep tracks to the village and the cox's bellicose voice recedes into the distance as the boat pushes away from us and the voice is gradually replaced by the warm, local sound of the Tvøroyri church organ.

Heidegger on the Beach

The last of the islanders

ON A DEW-SOAKED NOVEMBER night, the daylight long finished, I remember hearing a Faroese radio program about Svínoy (an island in the far north of the archipelago, close to Fugloy). Svínoy was the only island in the north that I had not yet visited. This time, in the summer, I made a point of going. Svínoy is a tiny, almost abandoned island of a few narrow by-lanes where pigs once wallowed in the mud. Now, in the winter months at least when it is lashed with foam, it is almost given over to nature. The island is a frontier, an outpost, a narrative symbol of exchanges and encounters. Such places have always had an inexplicable appeal for me; their absolute peripherality draws me in. There are just fourteen people that live on the island. Fourteen residents that sit alone in small, box-shaped dim-lit rooms browsing crumpled telephone directories to see who is still alive before retiring to cobwebbed bedrooms; the voices of the radio and the sea linger in their memories and connect them to other shores. Or at least, that is how I picture it. I imagine in the winter months the lone figure who lives next to the abandoned bible school walking down a thoroughfare of dusk partially lit by a metaphorical, flickering street lamp. He watches the night that moves in the streets and the sea that begins to see-saw. He walks silently past the lemon-colored houses whose corrugated iron casing is rusting away and onto the church where a famous Viking is buried in the grounds. He takes up his pew alone in the church trying to find dignity in his loneliness; the oldest Faroese language bible remains on the altar. He waits for the priest who is stuck out at sea in the swirl. Amidst all the myths and stories that linger in these near-empty places of worship, he prays for those residents who have drowned in recent storms. With him, there had never been any idle talk. No Heideggerian *Gerede*.

99

I disembarked from the small ferry called Ritan that serves these northern islands on one *fjallljóst* day – on one of those rare Faroese days when the weather was clear enough to go up into the mountains. I walk up the track that climbs slightly under knitted telegraph wires. Rusting farm machinery points to more productive days. In the short summer months, the wet fields and drainage ditches hum with the curious drone-like electric sounds of mating snipe. Camouflaged, they burst from their cover beside me and fly in a zig-zag pattern to evade predators.

On the narrow lane that leads up from the quay of the west coast of Svínoy, dumpy wrens (*músabróðir* 'mouse's brother') stand sentry on garden posts. Yards littered with corroding Dutch hoes have been rewilded by flocks of starlings whose metallic plumage shines in the morning sunshine. Wheezing and sputtering, they bring the island to life in clouds of noise. The males mimic an orchestra of bird calls, and collectively create a baffling acoustic confusion. At this time of the year in Svínoy, the empty lanes are decorated with aquamarine fragments of their egg shells. The lane rises further up from the shore, dividing agricultural fields with bales of hay, a solitary cow, geese and chickens. Svínoy is one of the few islands in the Faroes flat enough to permit baling. There is a dairy farm here, one of just a handful left in the Faroes. But no sign of people and no sign of pigs after which the island is curiously named, simply the oversized, unshorn sheep that graze on the beach and in people's gardens.

Juniper lines the tracks where tractors from the last century sit abandoned. Without any obvious explanation, dead fulmars have been strung up outside empty-looking homes. The lane winds around a trickling stream that meanders past late nineteenth century vernacular architecture. As is common for the Faroes, many houses have a name and a date (Á *heygnum* 'by the hedge', 1899). Just as in Kirkja, on the neighboring island of Fugloy, there used to be a strong community here. A couple of hundred perhaps. Now, you come here to find solitude and listen to the starlings chatter and purr. During the Candlemas storms, these islands might be cut off for weeks at a time. But with wind-dried mutton hanging in their *hjallar* and hens clucking all over the yard, this is of little significance. Subsistence is no stranger to the people that live on the most remote islands.

I walk the narrow streets and soon end up on the shore. A wordless, elderly farmer – an autodidact, as I later discover, with interests in Norse archaeology – walks the Svínoy shore metronomically. He scours the beach for messages in bottles written in the last century. And occasionally, he finds one. He stands silently, shuffling his thoughts. Clouds scud across the sky. Shadows hang under his eyes. His hair is wild, his eyes misty and his forehead is etched with tributaries of wrinkles. He has a serious, academic mien. A mood of loneliness travels across his face, but I suspect he likes to live on the outskirts of life. I wonder if acute shyness has brought him to Svínoy. Never banalities of sentiment, the bottles he seeks, these messages of love written to strangers have sometimes circumnavigated the globe several times, bouncing around in countless tides. Once they were pleas of help and despair from those spending their last days on the Scottish island of St Kilda and other liminal places. These maritime telegrams have been found in corked bottles on the beaches of the Faroes, Shetland and the Hebrides. They include everything from murder confessions, apologies, pleas for help from castaways, appeals for love from wayfarers and messages of longing. Shortly after I first spot him, I have joined him on the shore where he has his roots. We exchange a few syllables in the local dialect. He is imprisoned in his single words. It is some days since he last spoke. His tongue withers in his throat; his larynx creaks slowly into action, pushing the sounds through pathologies of phlegm. He divides his thoughts up into words. Local rounded vowel sounds. He gives me a half-smile, and then shuffles away from the interstitial shore resisting small-chat with a stranger. A few moments later and from the shoreline, his features can no longer be discerned.

These islanders of the north are often introverted; welded to the decrees of God, the lantern to their feet. He walks to the tiny village cemetery in search of ancestors hiding in tombs. The whole island is suspended in the void. Dialogue participants die one-by-one. Then he returns home, the house closest to the shoreline, to spirals of memory and his mute world, the company of the radio and yesterday's chores. Alone with the gods again and his private soliloquy. A servant of sorrow. He sits at home studying vanished alphabets and lingering over inessential melancholies. Amidst capsized chairs, he watches the barometer tick down and finishes genealogical puzzles. Solitary in the canary-yellow house, he spends his evenings reading from the Book of Deuteronomy.

In a bay near Fámjin on the island of Suðuroy, I found my own message in a bottle. A nine-year-old boy from Thurso, Scotland had sent it eight years previously. The crumpled message in a Pepsi plastic bottle was difficult to read. I traced patiently the faded script with a pen. It was not possible to read his name, but he had left the address of his school. He just wanted to say 'hello', to somebody out there. Later that evening, I wrote to the school to tell them about the message, but never heard anything back. Perhaps I should have put my message in a bottle.

On the other side of the island of Svínoy, there is a track that leads away from the village towards Fugloy. Once I have exhausted the rest of the island, I walk the last remaining track to see if I can find anything of interest, a new view or perspective at least. The track is wild and barren. Wheatears hop from one stone to another and a triumvirate of swashbuckling arctic skuas, the kleptoparasitic pirates of the North, twist and turn, harassing relentlessly an innocent oystercatcher like a World War II pilot. Their brusque, hectoring manner is unmistakable for they are so aggressive. As I rest by a cluster of boulders, heated by the sun, I catch a faint smell of boggy peat land. Then suddenly, from somewhere behind me, comes a great skua. The great skua does not have the pointed wings, long tail and patch of yellow below the nape that the arctic skua has. It is a larger, plumper bird, brown with white on the wings. Its plumage is not dissimilar to a buzzard. Unprovoked and fearless, the great bird attacks, flying right at me in a dive-bomb kamikaze attack. Unlike an arctic tern which will fly just above your head to warn you off, a great skua will aim to fly into you. They attack anyone and anything that gets close to their nest. I have clearly wandered into its territory and am thus fair game.

I could see its unswerving eyes, the detail of its massive mottled barrel chest and the lethal curved beak bent towards me. At the last moment, I threw myself flat on the ground. The bird flew just centimeters above my head, scraping across the back of my jacket. In shock, I picked myself up and moved quickly away from the rocks assuming a nest was nearby. The bird had turned in the sky and was coming back for me in the manner of a Japanese bomber on a crash-dive attack. I started to run. Once again, I dived onto the soft lichen just as it was about to hit me. I ran down the hill with the bird in hot pursuit, circling and then repeatedly lining up its attack. This last, untamed track would have to wait for another visit. I return to the huddle of houses near the shore, thinking how comical this spectacle must have appeared.

A silent, scarlet-faced farmer, his wheelbarrow full of peat, had paused to watch. Blood vessels had broken on his cheeks. An almost expressionless face painted by lost triumphs. I offer a half-hyperventilated account of the bird's aggression. But, it is not necessary. Brows raised, his sausage fingers clasp the cold metal of the wheelbarrow handles and he walks to the outfield without saying a word. I had come to an ephemeral island of dreams where few words were exchanged.

* * *

I listen to the early morning *andakt* (a psalm and early morning prayer) on the radio in Svínoy, pack my bags and close the door to the small, neighborless white house where I spent the night. I take the boat to the island of Fugloy which means literally 'the bird island'. This time, I head for the settlement of Kirkja and not Hattarvík where in a barely light December I had previously stayed. Now, it is July and climbing the steep slope leading up the jetty to Kirkja, it seems that the people have left and the animals have taken over. A Faroese horse dines on the remains of a cabbage patch. Border collies run towards me, and guide me proudly around their deserted village, checking over their shoulders occasionally to make sure I follow. This island lives up to its name: there are birds everywhere. Gulls sway on the up-winds; kittiwakes blown aloft.

Behind a confusion of nettles, I find the house where I am meant to be staying. Dead fulmars with cold, dark eyes hang from the fence, waiting to be plucked and boiled. The porch is full of unopened packages and discarded shoes. The door is open, but nobody has visited for a while. Half-hidden behind what appears to be a theatrical scrim, a man from a distant window on the other side of the lane watches the starlings roost. It is said that a neighbor threw himself into the sea out of loneliness.

I call Amalie, my host. *Å, noi, ikki hetta husið*...('oh, no, not that house') and then a plump figure squeezes out of a house a couple of tracks away, waving and shouting. Amalie wears her jacket off at the shoulders. A heavily-stained T-shirt partially covers her generous bulk. There are small spiders enmeshed in her long hair. Language falls out of her mouth in warm bursts. She is jolly, and has not the slightest concern for the goings-on beyond these islands. She knows Kirkja is almost forgotten, but does not care. This always has been home and she is content with her fate. I will be lodging with her for the night. The kitchen is chaotic. Legs of lamb are piled up on the worktop; drying sheep bladders hang from the ceiling. A radio plays rather too loudly. The living room looks out across the Fugloyarfjørður to Svínoy where I have just come from. The walls are hung with ill-framed black and white photographs of bygone days in Fugloy.

At the center of the most spectacular isthmus to the west of Kirkja sits the *bygd* of Viðareiði, brutally exposed to the storms that rage in the winter. Storms, so violent, they washed away part of the cemetery. Coffins, she tells me, were recovered in Hvannasund, six miles to the south on the west coast of the island of Viðoy. These islands are full of stories of itinerant priests, rushing from one tragedy to another. In the olden days, when a child was born it had to be baptized as soon as possible for so uncertain were a newborn's prospects. Men from Fugloy would often risk their lives by rowing to Viðareiði to see if they could find a priest. If the priest were not there, they might have to row a further half a dozen miles or so to see if they could find him in Hvannasund. Once they had found a clergyman, the husband and the priest would then have to try and row back and land on the rocky shores of Fugloy.

Amalie is one of only eight people who live full-time in Kirkja, but there might be forty houses. Many of the scabbed houses are empty, for much of the year at least, their net curtains discolored, their window sills garnished with dead flies. In total, the population of the island is about fifteen. We sit in the living room chatting. Describing the people that live here as a bit 'special', Amalie throws her head back and laughs heartily. *Ja, ja tey eru tað* ('yes, yes, they are that'). She looks out of the window to the green slopes edging down to the water onto the fastest current in the Faroes, and explains how you never tire of the view, how there is always something to do. 'Here, you have everything you need', she insists cordially. More fuzz on the radio. She is saddened that there are so far fewer seabirds now than there used to be, that the pods of whales that used to pass through the straits have become increasingly seldom. But, the view has never changed. It is wild, raw; subject to God's providence.

When life is slow and uncomplicated like this, time is measured by the simple events: the *andlát* ('the news of the dead') on the radio; the arrival of the boat, Ritan, three times a day; the ringing of the church bell on a Sunday; a visit from the lady-farmer in Hattarvík who greets Amalie's guests with a sunken smile. I am joined by two men who are visiting from Tórshavn to carry out repairs to the church. They slurp their tea audibly and are as fascinated by the near deserted island as I am. Sleeves rolled to the elbow, a community of three brought thither by different circumstances speculate about the priest that is coming on Sunday to hold the service. The last one that came ran off with a local girl, leaving a factory of gossip and tears of laughter for Amalie who regales the story repeatedly.

CHAPTER 3: THE FAROES

* * *

On Sunday afternoons after the Thomas Kingo psalms have been sung, a low deep monotone voice reads chapters of Faroese history on the radio, often about the war and the involvement of Faroese fishing vessels:

> 'During the war, many Faroese fishermen lost their lives, shipping fish and coal to Britain across waters that were bombed by the Germans and littered by sea mines'... 'Flying the Faroese flag, as ordered by the British (Denmark was occupied by Germany), the *Nýggjaberg* trawler went down off the coast of Iceland in 1942, killing twenty-one Faroese seamen'.

I sit listening to the radio in Amalie's living room. After the program, Mendelsohn's Hebrides Overture is played, and then I walk to the remains of various World War II bunkers in a trapezium of light. These islands have an out-of-the-way charm. In a world of microscopic digital discovery, you can find forgotten places here. They are as timeless as the black and white photographs on the wall with their smooth tonality. I wish there were more places like this. You never forget them. They are like metaphors. You feel mysteriously privileged. Occasionally, your mind will revisit them with acoustic flashbacks of oystercatcher peeping. Sometimes you wonder if you might want to die here. By cutting yourself off occasionally, you rediscover the joys of the simple, sensual life. Its wholeness. The sound of the sea; the sound of a voice.

Some islands feel remote, but Fugloy and Svínoy seem cut off. This is island life in all its sea-salted gritty minutiae. There is no fake language of intimacy here. Nobody is going to ask you how you are when the day is packed with chores. There are no glib answers to difficult questions. They are in a world of their own, a world of chimerical beauty sometimes concealed behind flung spray and brown spume. They live alone with their verbal play. Radios sit on the window-sills. The sea is always in the background; the colorful, slanted corrugated iron roofs of the houses all face the sea. The roofs are all at slightly different heights. Everything plunges towards the sea. The *hjallar* (one for meat, one for fish) are placed by streams or the sea to minimize the chance of flies getting to the meat in the summer. Then, there are the wild flowers, the roaming border collies, the rills that wend their way through the villages. But on both Svínoy and Fugloy, the balance has shifted over the course of fifty years or so from human to nature as the voices of dying bachelors have fallen silent.

When the radio dramas ebb into the silence of midnight, almost all the sounds are from the natural world. The near-abandoned houses that drift in the mist have more or less given themselves back to nature. Water seeps in through rotting window frames, purling down the back of tattered, torn leather sofas. Starlings nest in disused chimneys and congregate in larger numbers than usual. There is the occasional human voice. It is rather bird-like. But, you might have imagined it. There is a sense of exposure, of vulnerability. Some of the people are as wild as their surroundings. Others are incurably shy.

Amongst the clustered houses, there is a tiny *handil* ('grocery store') that looks like something from a century or so ago. Tins are stacked high; bottles of *Jolly* soda are lined up like soldiers on parade. You have to call in advance if you want it to open. Just beyond the *bygd* are the archaeological ruins of a once much more impressive settlement. It is clear that previously Fugloy supported a bigger community. Not far from the ruins, the present church dates from 1933. I am shown around by the same man who I met earlier. As we enter, it starts to rain, the heavy drops exploding on the window panes. The man is from Tórshavn, and was here last year too replacing the windows in the church:

'Fugloy, å, ja. It is a very special place to live. Ja, ja.'

He has piercing blue eyes and a gentle smile. His voice is sunken, the sounds pushed up from the bottom of his throat. The pews are unpainted; bare varnished wood. The walls are goldenrod-colored. There is an ornate, wooden roodscreen. And then behind the altar, between two oversized paschal candles in this most modest of churches in the farthest flung corner of the Faroe Islands, the magnificent Sámal Joensen-Mikines of Christ walking on water draws you in. Mikines, one of the greatest Faroese artists, grew up on the island of Mykines, a small island in the west of the archipelago known for its pink and grey shades of light when the sea and air melt together. The glowing figure is draped in white, pulling the disciple, Peter, out of the dark, angry swirl. In such a religious community where so many lives have been lost at sea, the symbolism must be deeply poignant. Moments later, the rain has run its course and the clouds sink below the valley with stoic resignation. Confident that I have seen everything there is to see in Kirkja, I retire to my small, overheated room in the loft and listen to the radio before bed. The sky is painted with purple, night clouds. I can hear the streams tumbling over rocks. I extinguish the lyrical radio voice and drift off to sleep.

Tunnels

A journey to meet a singer of Faroese ballads

A FEW MORE BENDS of the weary road, and fog like mystical smoke pours
into the valley, blotting out the Canada Geese flying past the car and smudg-
ing the occasional abandoned sheep house. And then we enter a tunnel.
The single-lane, unlit mountain tunnel is very narrow, dark and unnerving.
A ram grazes immediately above the semi-circular tunnel opening. Einar,
almost ninety now, is driving me to Sumba at the other end of the island of
Suðuroy. Einar has been telling me about the history of the island, its traditions and the old ways of doing things. We are going to meet Axel, a singer
of Faroese ballads and ring-dancer.

We enter the tunnel and are surrounded by penetrating blackness.
Everything is amplified: I can hear the mountain drip, I suddenly become
more aware of Einar's tinny voice as the hammers strike firmly the keys. The
engineers that built this tunnel toiled so hard for so few. There is nobody
here. The tunnel is one thousand five hundred meters long and connects a
village of fifty people with shared mannerisms and collective gaits. Shortly
after the boring of these first tunnels, tunnel-mania took hold and by 1980,
another seven tunnels had been built in the Faroes. It meant that the villages could all be connected, and the very windy mountain roads that were
barely navigable in the winter could be avoided. The Hvalbíngar, as the
people of Hvalba on the southernmost island are known, with their sharp
tongues and fiery wit protested that the tunnel would 'destroy our culture'.
They believed that people from Hvalba were different from the other villages on the same island, and they wanted to keep it that way.

Up until the 1960s, to visit another settlement, the Hvalbíngar would
have had to wait in pollock-smelling parlors for good weather before negotiating on foot the lips of their mountains. Then, when the tunnels were

built in the 1960s and 1970s everything changed. Now, the mountains were like wind instruments, perforated, pierced and punctured. Tunnel gossip would pass from A to B in a few damp minutes instead of wind-swept days: a Scot, a former convict on the run from Glasgow gangs, had an altercation in this tunnel, after refusing to reverse his car having gone past the drive-in bay. There was a hidden quarrel in a black, unlit tunnel on a remote island. The case went to court, and subsequently the Scot disappeared. Such private disputes can soon become public ridicule on small, gossipy islands. And indeed, the Scot's defense in court became public verbatim when jokes were shared in the only bar on Suðuroy. Every nook and cranny of this lilting landscape with its scuffed stones is in fact a story. The characters, the ballads, the words and the metaphors linger on the cliff edges, the openings of the tunnels, on the grassy hill and the rusting sloop.

Encased in black, damp rock, we speed through the dripping granite mountain. The darkness continues. I am reminded of Friedrich Dürrenmatt's story *Der Tunnel* where the tunnel never ends, and the passengers on the train are entirely unnerved. Suddenly, we reemerge from the tunnel to a curdled sky. The road swings sharply to the left and then snakes down the valley to the sunken settlement of Hvalba which lies towards the northern end of Suðuroy. Clouds are heaped above the wild, windy isthmus. The narrow piece of land in the middle is cruelly exposed to the elements. I am pleased it is as I remember. Nothing has changed. The cappuccino-colored Faroese horses with tilted hind hooves still stand amidst hay-drying racks and periscoped pillboxes – camouflaged, concrete dug-in guard posts built by the British when they occupied the Faroes during the Second World War. The horses turn their backs to the incessant wind that sweeps through the channel. Their gaze is melancholic; their long lashes the envy of any woman. A handful of men cluster around a shed chatting, holding scythes (*liggið*) and snaths (*orv*). The old ways work just fine here. We pull in and walk along the slate-grey beach. The beach is empty except for an occasional unhinged clam shell and a screeching inquisitive arctic tern that patrols the shore. Our footprints are the first and perhaps the last of the day. We listen to the coiled sea and my thoughts veer in the tide. There is a feeling of the world slowing down. I study the angles of the sun. The colorful Hvalba houses that line the bay at each end clash with the rims of the postcard-green isthmus, a psychedelic splash captured in the Zacharias Heinesen painting that hangs in the living room in my rented Tvøroyri house. Zacharias is a Faroese painter and son of the well-known writer,

William Heinesen. I met him once in an art gallery in Tórshavn. He can often be found in one the cafés looking out to sea. Einar and I talk about Heinesen as we circumnavigate the village. Clouds march across the sky in a frenzy; flashes of light and ephemeral beatific visions. Behind the beach, T-shirted, mud-spackled men rake rectangular, precious potato plots and chat about last year's crop. Alongside the plots, small trains of young girls whose husbands are away at sea push prams around the isthmus (*eiði*) along the empty roads. They acknowledge the visitors, and then return to their conversation.

Back in the car, Einar's spidery fingers grip the steering wheel. His voice adopts a warm, soft tone when he talks about the distant family he still has dotted around Hvalba: the second cousin once removed, the second cousin twice removed, the third cousin once removed. All called Helgi. The conversation turns to *rukkur* ('a clown like figure and caustic joker'). *Å, ja, rukkur, ja, ja, tað er mongir her í Hvalbi.* He laughs and grins. Hvalba is full of *rukkur*, he says. Most Faroese boats tend to have a *rukkur* on board. Hvalba is known for its light touch. In former days, *rukkur* were men with salty faces, calloused hands and ears tuned to hymns on the radio. Aboard boats in the 1930s, they would gather around the wireless amidst the telegraph traffic in the radio room. They lived their lives amongst half a dozen voices on trawlers in interlocking camaraderie; an ocean *esprit de corps* punching through brown spume.

Einar turns on the car radio. Hymns pour forth. The love of God's word is still to be found here. A local choir on the radio sing sanctities and speak of solemn sovereignties. Their voices are rich and alive. It is a Thomas Kingo hymn for the flotsam, for the mangled men who were washed ashore and made their home here. Kingo was a seventeenth century bishop, poet and hymn-writer. His melodies were used in the churches following the Reformation. The hymn finished, Einar tells me about Westerbeek which was a Dutch East India Company ship that ran aground on the skerries on the west coast of Suðuroy. All eighty men were rescued from that shipwreck in 1742. It is said that you can recognize the descendants of the crews shipwrecked on the Faroes because their hair is darker than most. I feel as if I have seen them sitting in the pews at church. In the not-so-distant past, many Faroese were killed at sea. Einar talks of how he still remembers their faces from years ago. Now they lie supine in the valleys of capsized dreams. When the sea snared the souls of men, their cargos washed up on the whispering shores. Others were never seen again. In some of the smaller villages, the widowed women still wait at the windows, wondering if they will hear their man's voice again and counting the hours of life. There is a silence; his voice slips into the abyss. Then, he starts to talk about nicknames. Everybody has a nickname in Hvalba. Sometimes several. 'There are no private men here', he tells me.

We drive back through the tunnels that we navigated earlier in the day. The darkness of the tunnels closes the world around us. Then a spray of light as a car enters the opposite end. Once you have passed the car in the drive-in bay, the trembling suspense of a pending, dark encounter soon returns. Leaving the tunnel, we weave through rural tableaux of weeping valleys, and the butter-cup meadows of May, moist with morning rain. Under skies of translated light, we cross naked hills to the southern tip of the island, Sumba. It takes about forty minutes to drive from one end of the island to the other. There is just one road. I had been to Sumba once before. On a chill December day. As with many place names in the Faroes, there was a lively discussion as to what the correct etymology of Sumba was. But the consensus was that it probably referred to the south-lying *bøur* ('in-field'), and thus *sør bøur* became Sumba. It is not a place you easily forget. It is a place you always want to go back to just to make sure that it is exactly as it was before. People have lived there since the seventh century, and not a great deal has changed over the years.

Emerging from the most southerly tunnel on the island that connects Sumba with Lopra (the tiny village before the tunnel with an early twentieth century Norwegian whaling station), the road winds down an undulating brae called Beinisvørð. The brae sits amongst bluffs of solitude and from a distance, looks like a wave beneath a sky of gulls. Unlike in Hvalba, the houses, many of them empty and dying, face the sea head-on and must be totally engulfed in the worst of the storms. Everything leads to the sea here in Sumba. You could come here just to look at the light bend, listen to the ocean heaving with spittle, and wait for the lighthouse on the antique peat landscape to blink.

Sumba is the Land's End. It is the end of the road. Sitting at the bottom of Suðuroy, it is where the currents meet at the edge of civilization. In this part of the archipelago, the ship-wrecked ocean is studded with perilous skerries that wait in the strong current called the Røstin. For centuries, lives were abbreviated on these rocks. Now, they are memories, evoked in songs, ballads and hymns. Sumba is known for the old way of life and for maintaining traditions. The old traditions live on in the dusty *dansistovan* ('a dance hall still found in most villages') and in the spumed rowing boats. Men still row out their sheep in May to graze on the islet of Sumbiarhólmur that lies just off the coast. A good deal heavier, they are then collected and slaughtered in September. The sublime voices of the Sumba men can still be heard thumping on the radio. Some of the best chain-dancers in the country are from Sumba. Siblings, Axel and Erli have lived their entire lives in Sumba and are known across the island for their oratory and knowledge of Faroese ballads. Erli is known as the local coiner of words. Well into their seventies, they shuffle, edging with posterity, down the only street in Sumba to meet us. We wait for them at the memorial to those lost at sea where old men come to philosophize in the slow rain. Most Faroese villages have such memorials, but this one is the most impressive I have seen. Decorated with briny wreaths, it reads like an anthology of shipwrecks. Axel talks us through the plaques, the names, nicknames and names of the houses where the drowned lived are engraved on a tapestry of silver plaques.

Those fallen fugitives all across the Faroes (not just in Suðuroy) fought with nature, the seasons of the wind, and not man. Many of those who drowned came from the smallest settlements, such as Sandvík. Sandvík sits on a horse-shoe shaped bay at the northern tip of Suðuroy. These Faroese men were often killed in the *grindadráp* where pods of pilot whales are duped onto the blood-stained beaches. The loss of these men was God's business, the siblings said. In earlier times, places like Hvalba were subject to less well-known Ottoman pirate raids, when Algerian pirates took Faroese people from their unlocked homes and sold them into slavery on the Barbary Coast. That was over three hundred years ago.

Axel and Erli are kind and generous with their time. They do not hesitate to give up an afternoon to a stranger. They invite us to their home and I am soon let loose on their bookshelves full of extensive compilations of obituaries broken down by profession. The smell of the books governed over all the other smells of the house. Well-thumbed registers listing Faroese lawyers, dentists, teachers and doctors record the place of birth, death and place of occupation for every practitioner. There is no anonymity here. Older directories showcase an album of hard expressions of lost childhoods fraught with poverty. There are books of poetry too with unusual words underlined in black ink.

We speak for hours about the subtleties of the Sumba dialect over pots of black coffee and plates of stale buns. Their stressed vowels are short and their pronunciation of ø sounds strange to my ear. Built like miners, these

two wise brothers speak in soft narratives filled with local color. They are
both lay-preachers at the church, storytellers and amateur taxidermists.
They occasionally burst into song, singing ballads full of ancient lyrics describing epic battles. They hammer out the archaic words and stomp their
feet. The rhythmical stomping of the feet with its medieval monotony bores
it way into your mind and leaves you feeling almost dizzy. These special
melodies in Sumba are not so recitative and have a wide range – up to one
and a half octaves:

> Árla var um morgnunin,
> Ið sól tók fagurt at branda,
> Tað var ungi Ásmundur,
> Hann lystir út at ganga

> Gyltan spora
> Við mítt fótaspenni
> So temji eg mín gangara góða
> Lætur renna

> It was early in the morning,
> The sun shining beautifully,
> There was the young Ásmundur,
> He wanted to go out

> A golden spur,
> With the buckle of my shoe,
> So I tame my good steed,
> And let him run

Then, they tell us stories about wayward cousins. A famous poet, Poul F.,
lived here, in the house painted a Byzantine blue, up on the hill, Erli says.
Axel and Erli talk stoically about the hardships of these ancestors. They take
turns to describe the events in the passive voice: 'it was known that in those
days men would walk many miles over the mountains, carrying a coffin to
the nearest church for burial'. The pall-bearers would stop occasionally to
sip from their hip-flasks and sing songs. The people of Sumba are learned
men and women. In former times when this settlement was much more
cut-off, visiting priests would come scrambling over the hills or land on the
rocky shores with liturgical texts and piles of scholarly books on all manner
of subjects. The Sumbiar, as the people of Sumba are known, would read
everything they could get their hands on, no matter how esoteric: botanical

treatises, philological monographs, Icelandic anthologies and philosophical memoirs. They chased knowledge relentlessly.

At the end of an enjoyable afternoon, we thank our hosts and make our way back to Tvøroyri as dusk inches down. The air smells of wet sheep. A sensory anchor, an olfactory anvil that makes you feel grounded. Technically, it was summer but the seasons really fluctuated. From day to day. Sometimes, minute to minute. On the way back, we drive through torrents of rain and pass rows of wooden houses with tin roofs, and spalled balconies partially eaten away by the salty sea air. And yet by the time we reach Tvøroyri, elderly farmers are to be seen walking down from the outfields in the afterglow of the sun.

Chapter 4: Sweden

'Who if I cried would hear me above the angels' orders?' (Rainer Maria Rilke)

Radio Fuzz
A mêlée à trois

RAGNAR – AN INTROSPECTIVE, retired lighthouse keeper – sat fiddling with the dial on the short-wave radio. Like the lighthouse, he had been de-commissioned. The higher-ups had a liking for technology, it seemed. His solitary, philosophizing work was no longer needed; trimming the wicks, replenishing fuel, cleaning lenses, winding clockworks. The trembling lanterns awash in mercury, the sound and smell of the engine room – they were just memories. And so, he had embraced resignation and returned to life in the woods where he listened to the radio when the weather was black and the days were short. He had been taken in by the voices. 'We are all automated now', he would mutter to himself as he gave the dial a nudge. Everything had changed, but his life alone with his radio and his jumbled memories lived on. He peers out of the window onto the northern land-scape. It is early evening and the two lit houses have become three. Almost a community. There have been local disputes. Talk is minimal between the three last residents of the village who sit in rooms kept alive by radio fuzz. Each sits at home, without verbiage. As the batteries began to wear down, they would sidle up to the radio craning their necks not wishing to miss a word. There was Ragnar, Einar and Ingmar. Ragnar and Ingmar had sparred over a visiting doctor to whom they had both taken a fancy to. Ingrid – a woman of class and quality of character – jilted them both and returned to her husband who lived in a far-away city.

From the window, Ragnar sees to the side of a field and in the distance, a lone man. Possessed by memory, Ingmar – a neighbor of sorts – wanders down an infinite, symmetrical logging track, almost hidden in thick, fresh snow. Ingmar – the verger since 1954 – moves confidently along the quiet country lane far from the urban geometry of streets. He meanders through a private cartography of the taiga, through battalions of birch and past moon-lit antique farmhouses. Ragnar listens for the gentle and familiar scrunch of Ingmar's boots in the fresh snow. It was years ago when they last spoke. Something dashes across the track in front of Ingmar, as fast as a fugitive prisoner: an arctic hare on the run through the arboreal mono-culture of spruce and pine. With the window ajar, Ragnar could smell the freshly cut wood. Stamped, bar-coded logs are piled up by the side of the track. 'Everything must have a number these days', he says under his breath disapprovingly. He liked neither the sound of machines nor the automation of society.

Back at home, the receiver was square and serious-looking. Spare bat-teries always on hand in the bottom kitchen drawer. When he sat alone in the lighthouse, he discovered that the reception was best just before sunrise but here at home the reception was better late in the evening. The tiniest ro-tation of the grooved silver knob, and he would be taken to another world: Ankara, Kiev, Sofia, Stockholm. There was a sense of achievement in land-ing the pin on the exact frequency; a sense of earnt peace to have beaten the cacophony of squeals that punched at his ears. Buffered by clouds of static, he would hover over the pin like a helicopter drifting between whims of atmospheric pressure. A nudge along the spectrum, and then new voices, forceful foreign sounds, overlapping speech, discursive violence. Ghanaian Pentecostalist prayers, news from Swaziland, religious zealots from a hilly country, Bulgarian priests, Lebanese football. Mysterious bleeps. All unfet-tered by intermediaries.

He grew to love this sense of audio discovery; the hunt for acoustic treasures entangled amongst the hissing and baleen like whistling. He nev-er knew how long the high-pitched whine and the crackling static would last for, what would come next, whether the idiom would be intelligible or totally unfamiliar. He would scramble through the spectrum of frequencies hunting for a lavish voice, the inaccessible languages – some articulated more urgently than others. The unknowns of shortwave radio were scat-tered before him, some of them barely audible, just traces of conversations that peter out into distant fuzz. Before bed, he would play with the dial to hear what was out there, surveying the acoustic landscape with the tun-ing pin. Who was speaking to whom, was it private, public or both? There was a sense of anticipation that came with the static, and then a distant voice could be heard in a hidden room in an unknown land. He wanted to find these people, this cradle of lonely, fragmented voices somewhere in the ionosphere to see if this was all real or some kind of fantasy acoustic theatre. There was a romance to it too, and a sense of mystery.

Sometimes shortwave met enigma, taking Ragnar into the domain of cold war shadows. A ghostly Russian military radio station would buzz every day – brittle and haunting – but its purpose remains entirely mysterious. A Russian voice reads out intermittently code words and numbers. Short wave radio enthusiasts tune in to hear the anomalous buzzing and fabricate elaborate conspiracy theories. A few more twists of the dial and then he hears an automated Stasi *Sprach* machine transmitted on three different frequencies simultaneously to confuse the jammers. Akin to some kind of frenzied Bingo, a child's voice reads out groups of numbers in muffled German. Ragnar would sit listening to these peculiar announcements, allowing the geography of his spirit to broaden.

The radio voice would take him back to the places he had been, the places that meant something to him, the encounters whose voices he never forgot. But, also to the cities labelled above the frequencies that he had only known acoustically. Radio frequencies became clotted circuits of memory built on a musical pell-mell of voices and idioms.

The fascination was with the voices, their individuating features, foreign words and the places they inhabited. He had always loved words, words that were not his own; the most precious ones were always those just beyond his comprehension, those that were just beyond his reach, shielded by enigma. He wondered why he had this sensitive acoustic memory that harvested voices, intonation patterns, accents and dialects in a rich, mental discography. Perhaps it was all those years surrounded by the swell of the sea, in those remote places killed off by loneliness. These transcendental voices came alive during those moments when alone he was caught between the ephemeral worlds of past and future. He was convinced there was something special about the radio voice. The voice was disembodied, but at the same time it imparted an authenticity. There was a strong human connection too. It was just a voice, but sat alone in the lighthouse the stranger behind the voice could have been sat next to him. The voice led him to conjure up memories of the endless onslaught of the sea. His imagination flourished. This textual soundscape would stream through his mind as he lay beneath the duvet in the final moments of the day.

Each Easter, sat alone in the keeper's house (before it was demolished) on that crumbling edge, that remote outpost, he would inch the knob towards a Russian short wave radio station that hid somewhere beneath the peeling Leningrad label. On this occasion, he would move the pin with a clear sense of purpose, not in the pre-bedtime exploratory manner. He had discovered the Russian Orthodox Easter Liturgy Mass on the radio. It had become a calendar event, an appointment with something mysterious. For several hours, his mind would be swept away across the Russian taiga with the spiritual imperatives and angelic melismas of this tremendous occasion.

Not stirring far from home now that he had retired to his childhood village in the north, he continued to discover the world through the radio voice. Sitting alone at the end of winter, he sat listening to the keening noise of the wind, to those distant voices projected into his parlor and the hours would slip by unnoticed. Suddenly, he recognized the chirpy radio voice from Stockholm. He remembered the distinct delivery and crisp consonants from a previous winter's slow evening. There was something singular about the voice. It was sharp and sincere; feminine and precise. The familiar voice introduced the next piece of music, *Cantus Arcticus: Concerto for birds and orchestra* by Rautavaara where he blends orchestral sounds with his own recordings of birds made sitting in the bogs of Lapland.

He listened to the bird song interacting with the orchestra. At this time of the year, the haunting sound of migrating whooper swans filled the room. Looking out of the window assessing potential visitors, he would watch them land effortlessly in flocks on the frozen fields opposite, carrying the souls of poets. Each year they would arrive just when winter winds down towards the end of March. Foraging in the melting snow, white-on-white, these swans evoked immortal longings and seemed to come from some kind of imaginal world of eternal peace. The dreamy aura of their legend was almost palpable, particularly on snowy days such as this.

Whilst listening to the Rautavaara piece, he looks out upon the land of his childhood that was now as hard as iron. His gaze sweeps across the abandoned, silent gardens that were still unfenced. He loved that graveyard feel of winter. Like clockwork, the *dimma* creeps through the wood in the gloaming of the day. A blanket of smoke tip-toing across the hushed fields, that are no longer yoke-colored, but stiff and glassy. The fog-scape envelops the blushing houses, one-by-one, overwhelming the abandoned seesaw, merry-go-round and trapeze rings amidst all the ambiguities of late afternoon. The next movement of the Rautavaara piece begins and his attentions shifts to a migrating Crane duet. Haunting and reverberating, they trumpet, side-by-side on the frozen sloughs. Here, the cranes can still play King and Queen. Their long, serpentine necks appear bodiless above the mist. Their stentorian squark torpedoes the silence, reminding him that we are alive. They are a mating pair brandishing their old-fashioned monogamy, amidst the ghostly lights of unbaptized souls that seek the holy water. A secular wind blows the latest snowfall from the roofs of empty churches. He thought he heard a telephone ring or perhaps a knock at the door. Distant seagulls mewl, free of the curse of perpetuity, and the sounds of the Rautavaara piece merge with the bird calls outside.

Ragnar goes out into the cold where the words are swallowed. His memories are drawn out of the shadows, repudiating and loving the same thing over and over again. Under snow-laden drooping pylons, he walks through the dying village to see if there might have been any talk. Anxious to avoid an encounter, Ingmar closes the door to his out-house and goes back inside when he sees him. Einar who sits alone in the kitchen, reading the Psalms, draws the curtains. The radio crackles and hisses. All three of them shift between the world of silence and sound, and then move back to silence. Red painted houses, lamplit and with white window frames, garnished with oversized, grey satellite dishes like elephant ears, dot the white landscape. There are boundaries, but not English ones with stiles and signposts, and with snow everywhere are rendered less relevant. There are no footpaths here. Instead, solitude lingers in meadows lost in snow. But, it was here, before the disputes, in these very quiet places that he remembered the kindness of strangers, here in the snowy evenings that withdraw into sepia faintness. It was in this village of memories that people went about their business quietly far from the ravages of the machine-worshippers. A visitor to Ragnar once observed how the few inhabitants had such solid substance behind their calm demeanor. They were able to affect others pro-foundly through the use of remarkably few words. That was the Nordic way. Ragnar knew that for sure.

With the fading light, the snowy forest exudes a haunted beauty. An unstalled horse stands alone in a field of snow, at the frontier of sleep. The scene might be set to Szymanowski's *Stabat Mater*, keen to reflect the hon-est, simple faith of peasants. The images are monochromatic, timeless. That moment on the empty, snowy road, when Ragnar thought he was com-pletely alone, suddenly a vintage Saab with a two-stroke engine appears in the distance. A stranger comes over the hill and breaks the solitude. The stranger waves knowingly. It feels like embracing an archaism, a piece of nostalgia.

The heavy snow hanging on the trees conjures up a circus of animal shapes. He loved the snow and all the mental images that brought life to the mind, the topography of imagination, that circulated in his thoughts. He clambered over the branches of his past. In the monochromatic winter, his eye focused on the shape, texture and overall meaning of the image. The frigid air leaves his mind sharp and awake. Everything seems clear somehow. Memories transmute into something closer to reality. He could see again the people that meant something in his life. He remembered his life in the lighthouse behind a wall of raging white foam.

A few tracks and roads lead through the forest, but otherwise the footprint of man is minimal. Occasionally, car headlights blinking through the spruce, illuminate the snow-laden trees. The sky can be thistle-pink for much of the day. At night, it might be smudged in fifty shades of green as the northern lights - the souls of stillborn babies according to the Inuit - dance and wobble.

He parades pass the puffballs in the busy wood. He is alone with his winter benedictions. He hears the voice of the wind. He listens to the language of the trees, the garment of vapor and breath. Here, there was no language of technology: the automated voices of talking lifts, reversing lorries and closing doors. He preferred a personality; liked to hear the clocks tick. He loved it in fact. Occasionally, he would walk through a speechless glade in the graveyard of the night. Sometimes he would walk along lonely logging tracks that divide the horizon so decisively with their linearity, and then down snowy tracks under a pewter sky that is *everywhere* in late afternoon. He knew that there would come those days where he would be content watching the birds all day long.

Soon, he would miss the radio voice and would return to the house of language, the mists of his inner monologues. He sat alone, animating his interior speech, following his own private thoughts. At every solstice and at every equinox, he was busy summoning up his memories one by one. He liked the harmonious succession of the seasons; all that ancestral memory. The spectacle of the world could only be his own. His language – by virtue of its own arrangement – could sustain a sense. Often, he could hear the words with singular clarity even after his late evening consciousness had ebbed away into the frustration of unremembered dreams. It was a kind of acoustic longing. The radio play would come to an end. The sleet would have become snow again. Pip, pip and then radio fuzz; the commotion of noise. Honeyed tones, a crackle, and then the sound of more radio static.

At this late hour, he might peek through the window and find his silent reflection – Ingmar looking back at him through his binoculars.

By the time the radio drama comes to an end, it is midnight. In the forgotten, frozen world at least. He loved the quietness of these winter evenings. Alone in the woods, the mind indulges in the fantasies of daydreams. He felt as if these moments belonged to him. At home, a warm voice speaks slowly. Rhythmically. *Dagens Dikt* plays on the radio, that rich five-minute slot that provides the perfect poetic ending to each day. *Dagens Dikt* has been running since 1937 on Swedish radio. He revels in its continuity. The voice is extremely slow; almost a burlesque of a rural vernacular. When life is slow, there is time to appreciate the music of every word. And where people live close to the land, the voices of men and nature can merge on blustery afternoons. He wondered who else is listening, who makes up this late-night acoustic community, spinsters perhaps scattered across the silent woods sitting in curtained rooms, drifting off to sleep. Occasionally, he would spy on Ingmar. Using his binoculars, he would find him sitting in the kitchen late at night alone with his radio. He would watch how he might start to shake or bang the radio if the kitchen became swamped in static or if the batteries started to fade.

But even radio programs far more mundane than *Dagens Dikt* flirt along the crease of poetics and music, he thought. He would listen to the private words read publicly, and absorbed privately. The softness of nightfall. The words read by a man sitting alone in a studio late in the evening somewhere in a suburban apartment perhaps, he speculated. He pondered the unseen intimacy of all this. *Dagens Dikt* is the musical transcendence towards the silence of the night. The velvety voice lingered in the architecture of his mind. It filled the room entirely with its emotional, hypnotic charge and instantaneity. He loved how the radio lent itself to these private moments with its intimacy and immediacy. Listening to the radio in the silence of the room at the dead of the night his mind was alive to every aural nuance. 'The radio was made for the poetic and for the ideological', he said aloud peering behind the curtain wondering when Ingmar would want to talk. He had always believed this.

Ragnar cherished those last few moments of the day when there is absolutely nothing but radio noise, when language again embraces the entirety of reality and experience. A private use of words is reserved for the most private part of the day. 'How often does somebody read aloud to you these days in this fashion?', he asked himself. These simple pleasures can be so rich when the indulgence is shared, or so he thought.

What Ragnar sought was those special moments when we are governed entirely by words again. Those final hours when you can scale the altitudes of imagination, and the words regain their resonance. He wanted to drift in their spores. He waited for those moments when language might eke out the lost powers of incantation, rediscover its rhetorical wealth, the corners of the day when he and the few remaining souls in the village might momentarily return to some kind of antique thinking. Slowly, he would edge into the citadel of privacy, the aura of complete stillness and the house of sleep. His consciousness would slip into that greater world. As night proceeded and time dissolved, he turns off the radio and returns to the world of dreams.

Then, there is a knock at the door. Ragnar gave a sudden start. His back shoots upwards with the nervous energy of a jack-in-the-box. He clutches the bed sheets, his head jerks to the left and the right seeking elusive answers. 'But, who, who could that be at this time of the night?', he asks in vain. The knocking continues, irritable and insistent. There weren't many options. It had to be either Einar or Ingmar. Both seemed implausible and filled him with disconcertion. Could he ignore it and hope it would go away? The knocking continued, more vigorously than before.

A face full of alarm, Ragnar gets up knowing it would be wicked to play dead, dons the bathrobe and makes his way tentatively to the hallway. He opens the door. A flurry of snow trespasses the threshold. All is still. There was a moment with nothing inside it. Before him stood Ingmar in his dressing gown. Ingmar gives him a disarming smile. He holds a transistor radio in his hand. He has aged. His hair turned white pointing in all directions in wild rebellion; eyes long buried in their sockets; back hunched over. The skin around his eyes had turned purple. There was a quiver in his voice. His speech belonged to a mournful dirge. Ragnar listens to Ingmar's words rise and fall. The disarming smile becomes a half-smile; almost earnest and imploring. An olive branch? Ingmar raises the radio as if it might be an offering of peace:

'Ragnar, do you have any spare batteries?' 'Please'. 'It is just that Einar has left for the town'. He said something about it was time to 'create a clean heart and renew a loyal spirit'.

Jam

A family affair

It was that time of the year when people made jam and swam in the lakes. However, he thought June was the best month to explore the back country. And so, they departed on a journey with an uncertain itinerary. The road was dead-straight, ascending slowly in the far distance. The empty spaces on the pale maps became larger as they headed due north. These wild places cannot be compressed into sheets of paper, thought Erik Ridderhjem, a handsome man who had made his money in newspapers, as he handed the map to her. They were on his way to his childhood home for mid-summer, but had chosen the most circuitous route possible. At home, there would surely be those torturous discussions and he needed time to think. It had been a pilgrimage of love and passion, but also a journey of almost forgotten memories. His fiancée sat beside him. Sophia was tall and svelte, but from different stock entirely. She wanted more than anything to be in the sticks, and this journey through the quietest parts of Sweden was tailored for her.

She marveled at the forests of birch on either side of the road that seemed to go on forever. As the North became the Arctic, these trees eventually became shrubs, shaped by the four winds of the sky. Valleys sunk beneath spangled veils of cotton grass. Her appetite for wilderness sharpened. Above the tree line awaited a vast apron of igneous rock with rounded mountain tops speckled with what she imagined to be snow. The rocks were painted green and ochre:

'Map lichen', Erik said before she could formulate the question and without a hint of doubt in his voice. There was a rasping finality to his tone.

He always spoke in that special clipped voice when he was stressed or preoccupied. He had had an English education:

'Obviously several thousand years old', he continued in that assertive, unchallengeable tone of his.

As they drove, Erik would identify all the birds they passed. One by one, and barely glancing at them for more than a second or two. He did not intend on impressing her, but was just doing what he did as a child when sat in the back being driven through the 'empty country' by his reticent parents. Tottering amongst the heather was the comical willow grouse with its self-ridiculing call. Bar-tailed godwits and golden plovers, the fell police, offered a duet from the side of the road. Marsh marigolds grew by rushing streams. A fence ran for thirty miles, separating reindeer herds. Sheltering from skuas, dotterels and turnstones patrolled the border. These names were meaningless to her:

'Skewers, dot-your-all and then turn to stone', she repeated with a quizzical brow as if he were speaking another language.

'Some people think this land is empty', he would repeat occasionally, 'but it is brimming with life', his sweaty hands grasping firmly the steering wheel.

They spent some days exploring the tundra. Herds of reindeer moved across the mountains in a shock of rain. A storm floated in the air. Prior to the storm, they sat amongst the heather listening to the sounds of the open spaces: the rhythm of the herd, their grunting and breathing like agitated cattle, the tinkering of bells, the flowing of the streams. The tundra felt immense. She sat in awe of the prodigious play of light on the horizon. Empty, except for a caravan of reindeer. She felt rewired.

The journey to the south to Erik's parents was long and uneventful. It was three days of endless birch before they arrived at the family estate where the preparations for mid-summer were being made. Mid-summer is celebrated in the Swedish countryside of Falun red wooden houses set against green meadows and gardens set alight by hollyhocks. In gardens full of purple lupines and bishop's lace. In this pagan hand-me-down, families gather to eat pickled herring and potatoes outside on long wooden tables. The food is washed down with beer and ice-cold *akvavit* from ornate shot glasses. The tastes of summer. Butterflies flutter in veils of ochre; sapphire dragonflies with transparent wings sneak up on the little boys telling lies. Little girls wear flowers in their hair. The sound of their cheerful giggling is heard in the tiniest of *landsby*. And there is much singing every time one raises a glass. Decorated with greenery and flowers, the maypole, symbol of fertility, is raised and the dancing begins. Followed by games.

Unmarried women pick flowers, and dream of a future husband. Or at least, that was Erik's recollection of mid-summer. It had been many years since he celebrated mid-summer in Sweden at the estate. Things must have changed a bit, he speculated aloud. He was occasionally harassed by writhing memories.

As always, Erik's mother was perfectly coiffed. Her mane of grey leonine hair swept back from her brow. She was in her early nineties, but spry and alert. Her chin was aristocratic, her nose straight-edged, her eyes twinkled and hinted at stories of a reckless youth:

'Oh, so you must be Sophia' she said looking away disapprovingly. Sophia was not the kind of woman to give way to despair.

His father was a shadow of his former self. His glazed eyes were buried in their recesses, his voice was quivery and his thoughts mumbled. He paid Sophia no attention whatsoever. Many people wondered 'but what if… then, what? Would his affairs be left in confusion?' If only the *if* were an if, thought Erik. They had never missed a mid-summer celebration at the estate, but now his parents exchanged few words. The pattern of conversation was so predictable, words were no longer needed. Decades of married years and their conversation had dried up completely. This year, the gathering was smaller than usual. Elderly aunts had sent their suspect apologies. But, the *akvavit* was flowing and with each glass the toasts and stories got longer and increasingly muddled. The old conflicts would surely surface soon, thought Erik. There would be talk of money and inheritance. Would there be any conditions to Erik's inheritance? The prospect of a left-handed marriage? Succession rights, entailed property? Erik feared as much. A little anxious, he tried to wind the alcohol-fueled party down prematurely by offering to take some of his nieces and nephews foraging for chanterelles in the forest. Those less familiar with the art of identifying mushrooms picked tart lingonberries instead. Some of the more sober ladies walked in the forest just to smell the pine.

In the coming days and only once the formalities had passed and any necessary conversations were subtly suppressed, the couple left the estate and stayed instead at one of his aunt's summer cottages. As a child, Erik used to go there to fish, walk in the forest, make jam and swim in the lake. His parents went there to find peace, enjoy some freedom from the estate's endless chores and see nature come alive again after the long winter.

Now, he came as an adult with his latest love. They spent their days swimming, *nu*, in the empty lakes. He always chose the most elusive one, hidden at the end of a logging track, navigated listening to a Beethoven sonata. He wanted them to have the lake entirely to themselves. The water was indecently cold, but he would do his best to persuade her to join him. With painful grimace, she would stand rigid like a statue with the water at thigh-level. He kept egging her on, reminding her that the longer she shied away, the less likely she would embrace it:

'Come on, join me. It is character building', he would shout and laugh splashing in the cold water like a carefree child. He splashes his face: a sensation of coolness, release.

She saw it slightly differently. Listening to his every word, she would ever so slowly muster up the courage to lower her body into the lake. Her legs were sent into a ritual shiver. Once she had made the plunge and after a few uncontrollable gasps for air, the memories of the cold would soon dissipate, he kept telling her. After some days of this routine, she finally admitted that these dips could almost become refreshing like the draught of morning air after a long sleep.

In the still lake, the ripples of concentric circles seemed to last forever in the endless summer sun. They swam alongside one another in a squall of tangerine light. The sound of splashing water in the silent lake echoed slightly. She circumnavigated the wobbly raft that served as a *point de repos* for swimmers, and then made again for the modest beach. Rising out of the water, she waded ashore. He sat watching her mesmerizing beauty *in toto*, and felt the luckiest man alive. The present moment was full of richness.

Sat between his legs and with a slight shiver, he would dry her hair, and then kiss the nape of her neck. She laughed at the goose bumps that would appear on her arms. The hairs on the back of her neck rose. And then her soft voice: she spoke with a mannered humility. He wanted to wake up to it every morning, and fall asleep to it every night. They spoke in that little language that lovers use and dried out under the midday sun, buckled to one another like perfectly dovetailed joints. She lay clasped in his longing arms. He wished he could capture this moment, and put it in a jam jar so that he could delve into in subsequent weeks and months like forbidden candy. Their kisses, seals of love, and warm embrace was only interrupted by occasional glances upwards at the empty sky, impressive for its lack of human interference. But then the telephone rang. Erik made for a forlorn figure, frowning and whispering into the telephone something about changes to his father's will as he paced up and down the beach, his shadow chasing after him. He returned, looking pale and quickly dismissed the call. He bore an expression that was slightly troubled. He wanted to push away his thoughts.

Occasionally, he would look at his watch scrutinizing the seconds hand in vain. His pulse quickened and time inched on.

They scribed love messages in the sand, and stayed until they could see their short summer shadows silhouetted in the water, washing up at dusk at gone eleven. Driving home barefoot beneath saffron skies, the feeling of the sand between his toes reminded him of a distant childhood. At home, they would exchange sonnets in chambers of the evening sun and make love under a pearlescent all-night glow in the white nights of summer. They would listen to Sunleif Rasmussen's Ólavsøka cantata on St. Olav's day, and think of the ocean on long evenings with faces dappled in shadows. Their happiness was only interrupted by the occasional phone call. He started to look at his watch, and wondered if the burden of time might start to encroach on their privacy.

In the endless days of summer, life slowed down to the point that they had no idea what day it was, whether the clocks had changed, whether they locked the front door. Patience became part of their daily routine again. The seasons were all they needed. That was the real time. The weather was the only deadline. The time punctuated by weather, light and darkness, and not appointments, the ringing of telephones or the buzz of alarm clocks. They began to perceive the passage of time through the alternation of day and night. After all, she wanted him to escape from the tyranny of the institutions tied to the clock. At the summer cottage, they had the time to ponder past events, memories, hopes and ambitions. They had time to think again.

Sprawled out on the chaise-longue, they drifted in and out of sleep on one of those timeless afternoons, remembering a previous summer. Behind glass, the warmth of the sunshine was soporific. The last rays of sun bounced off the window. It became a fight to stay awake as splendid images of the past resurfaced. Outside, charms of bullfinches colonized the young conifers that had started to grow again. Magpies haggled by the side of the road. The wind blew through the silver birches, the ghosts of the woods with flaking bark. It sounded like a distant ocean washing up a flotsam of memories. In his aunt's summer cottage, he liked to abandon himself to the voluptuousness of endless dreaming. On the scale of grand opera. He liked to take the time to play in the scaffolding of his dreams.

As he slept, he remembered the image of her. She lay straddled between his thighs. Her shapely curves mirroring those of the bathtub. He sung her a Swedish ditty. Softly, in her left cocked ear. He could not quite remember the words. But, almost. The slopping and splashing of the water. There was something soothing about the sound; meditative and touches the soul somehow. It echoed in the large, sparsely furnished room. He studied the maps on her hands. And, then he washed her hair. That long beautiful hair. He had examined it, strand by strand, on long summer afternoons sat on deserted beaches. She would toss it around when entering a room full of cocktail glasses, canapés and men dressed in Saville Row suits. It would tumble and land with an inviting grin. Submerged in the hot water with her, there was no tense, no mood. Nothing was conditional on anything. The past, present and future did not matter much. It was just being with her; a timeless gift. He swooned over her that summer. Time was measured by co-presence, and then the times apart that had their own chronology. That was what he sought, a space where time might unfold differently and where he would not be afraid of thinking.

The heat of the water clouded the ornate mirror, made her eyes twinkle and her bosom thump. Puccini's Tosca played from an upstairs room: emotive pianissimos and explosive fortes. Outside, twilight menaced the land. Shortly after they had retired for the evening, the telephone rang. He shuddered, wrenched unapologetically from sleep:
'Erik, my dear. It is mama. You must come home immediately. Papa has had a stroke. The doctor says he might not live until the morning. There are papers to sign'.
Sophia overhears the conversation. She places her hands on his cheeks, so that she can look him straight in the eyes:
'Erik, my dear, what are you going to do? Are you sure you want to get into this jam?'
'I have chosen you, Sophia. I have chosen you, not love according to a bond. I cannot heave my heart into my mouth'.

* * *

Erik drove to the estate alone. He spent the journey reorganizing the order of the words long since agreed upon in his mind. There were to be no renegotiations of intricate details, no obstructive filibustering and no sleight-of-hand.

Chapter 5: Armenia

'I will attempt day by day, to break my will into pieces. I want to do God's Holy Will, not my own' (Gregory of Narek)

Lady Yerevan

A Christian spirit

THERE WAS A SLIGHT nip in the air now that summer was drawing to a close. On the odd evening, the wind started to blow cold from the biblical mountains that encircled the city. Looking out over the sacred peaks, the hotel had previously been the Italian consulate in Yerevan, and occupied a favorable location in the city center.

She had been born under the shadow of Mt. Ararat in a run-down apartment block on a quiet street where storks build their nests on telegraph poles, and wore her faith around her neck. She was born in the century before last. Nobody quite knew her exact age, but what was certain was that she had been at the hotel for fifty-five years. Locals and visitors alike thought of her as Lady Yerevan, and called her such. Some chose to stay at the hotel on account of her good name alone. Well into her eighties, her contemporaries had long since withdrawn from this world believing it had little more to offer whereas Lady Yerevan's disciples continued to flock to her.

Despite standing at just under five feet tall, she had the looks and grace of a 1940s film star. You could imagine her being a hit on the vaudeville circuit. Her hair was always beautifully arranged, her mahogany-colored eyes sparkled between long lashes and her smile was electric. She dressed simply, but wore her clothes with a quiet distinction. She spoke in a friendly tone of voice that conveyed kindness and empathy. As a visitor to the hotel once noted, when a guest addressed Lady Yerevan the Christian spirit looked back at them: meekness and the practice of humility. She entertained a humble opinion of herself and was bound to a wise simplicity. There was an attractive modesty to her demeanor. To a guest who had once been rather short with her following a disagreement on the authorship of an eighteenth century sonnet, she replied: 'Sir, I know your compassion and the bounty of your kindness will exceed any iniquity'.

She took pains to make sure the guests had everything they required. She would usher them into the drawing room (which served as the hotel reception) in the manner of an attentive butler. She would then take the trouble to escort the guests to their rooms before returning to the drawing room where she would play patience.

Some guests were non-plussed to see such an elegant woman with an aristocratic air running errands, sweeping the steps, polishing the brass knocker early each morning and the like. It seemed unfitting.

The drawing room was somewhat higgledy-piggledy with late eighteenth century *bonheur du jour* practically piled up in one corner, and Louis XV commodes and George III antique secretaries wrestling for attention in another. The smiles of ancients recumbent on divans and framed men glowed at the visitors. Foreigners congregated in the drawing room: Italians, Russians, Germans, Frenchmen and Englishmen were seen to be poring over volumes of poetry. The room was a portrait of a lively mind. Men of letters came from afar to chat with Lady Yerevan and perhaps browse the books. One look at Lady Yerevan and her plush surroundings and they took her to be a writer of some renown. Books written in a multitude of languages lined the walls and were displayed in nineteenth century French empire walnut *bibliothèques*. Lady Yerevan's greatest hospitality was always reserved for writers who were allocated the suite on the Clementino wing should they wish to stay the night. Her questions to said guests were always much to the point: her genial, almost naïve smile disguised an intellectual shrewdness. Her erudition was prodigious and in her spare time she always had her nose in a book.

Lady Yerevan would pop out now and then to get herself a few odds and ends, but was otherwise absolutely wedded to the hotel. 'I really have no idea what they should do without her', acquaintances of hers were wont to repeat. She desired, however, no praise.

Lady Yerevan was seldom alone in the drawing room. Any number of intelligentsia would drop in and play bridge before soliciting her opinion on this or that. And, then there was Arpi who was privy to all kinds of abstract, intellectual discussions. In her mid-twenties, she was to all intents and purposes responsible for anything that might be deemed 'technical' to use Lady Yerevan's parlance, i.e. the paying of bills, the sending of telegrams etc. She was a trifle sullen and had been idle at school. Some thought it high time she was married. At first sight, she was not prepossessing and it was clear that unless she was very careful she would soon develop an unbecoming corpulence. However, she had a frankness which made people take to her and she felt as if she had a connection with Lady Yerevan. Arpi excited Lady Yerevan's sympathy. She had been on a few dates with a trader of apricots, but it seemed it would never amount to anything for she could not tolerate his roving eye. Lady Yerevan didn't have the heart to pry any further, but wanted more than anything else for the girl to find happiness and solace:

'That's neither here nor there, Lady Yerevan', Arpi would declare shrugging her shoulders if she dared speculate whether Arpi was currently courting or not:

'I am afraid I will never have anything of your glamour, Lady Yerevan. I am just a run-of-the-mill girl from the village whereas you have enjoyed undoubtedly chains of admirers all your life. You are the talk of Yerevan. Each day, I hear a new story! Whereas me, well, I suppose someone might take me off the shelf at some point', she continued with the corners of her mouth turned downwards. She aspired so much to be like Lady Yerevan, but lacked any worldly ambition.

Lady Yerevan had never married. She had always believed that ancestry was an impediment to the social life.

It was late summer and the busiest season of the year was beginning to wind down. As always, there were visitors for Lady Yerevan: retired diplomats, esteemed clergy, prize-winning poets etc. Despite this, she made the time to nurse a young lady from Milan who had been confined by indisposition to her bedroom. The Italian guest was touched but also surprised that a woman of such standing should lower herself to menial tasks. Lady Yerevan would bring her a cold flannel and rest it on her brow whilst reading Fausta Cialente aloud to her.

A Danish couple, natty in appearance, were also staying at the hotel that September. He was a scholar of Gregory of Narek and had come to Armenia to consult manuscripts at the Matenadaran. His wife was an artist of some repute. The couple had heard a great deal about the magnanimous Lady Yerevan and her vast learning. They had been assigned the

Clementino wing. At the end of their stay, they left the key on the Dasson gilt-bronze desk in the drawing room as guests were accustomed to do.

Lady Yerevan sat quietly in the drawing room, engrossed in a Balzac novel. Khachaturian's piano sonata played on the radio. Whilst she read, she held in her right hand a prayer rope and whispered the Jesus Prayer as she slowly rotated the bracelet, her index finger moving from one obsidian bead to the next:

'Excuse me, Lady Yerevan', said the Danish scholar in a raised voice thinking the elderly lady might be hard of hearing. His voice quivered slightly for he was not in the habit of speaking with such *grande dames*. He had prepared beforehand a phrase or two and practiced it in front of the mirror. He looked down at the chic, sophisticated lady sat on the Regency mahogany chair with her head in a book and thought her to be every bit a bluestocking:

'Oh, I do beg your pardon. I didn't see you there, Sir. It was quite amiss of me'. Lady Yerevan stood and with a broad smile looked up at the Dane who towered over her.

'I just wanted to say, Lady Yerevan, that we have had such a wonderful stay at your hotel', the scholar began as he craned forward. 'We should certainly like to return. Packed with first editions from floor to ceiling, our suite would, I am quite sure, upstage any first-class library that you care to mention'. There was a slight tremor in his voice as his throat dried up completely: 'Your hotel is really, erh…a historical gem, an absolute erh…one-off and it is a great honor for us to become acquainted with the owner of such a delightful establishment'. He turns to his wife so as to gain her approval for his nervous speech. She nods in emphatic agreement. There was a flicker of amusement in Lady Yerevan's twinkling eyes. She smiled, raised her right hand to her heart as if imploring forgiveness and said:

'Oh, I am not the owner, but a charwoman. You are mistaken. The owner is Arpi's father and lives two streets away'.

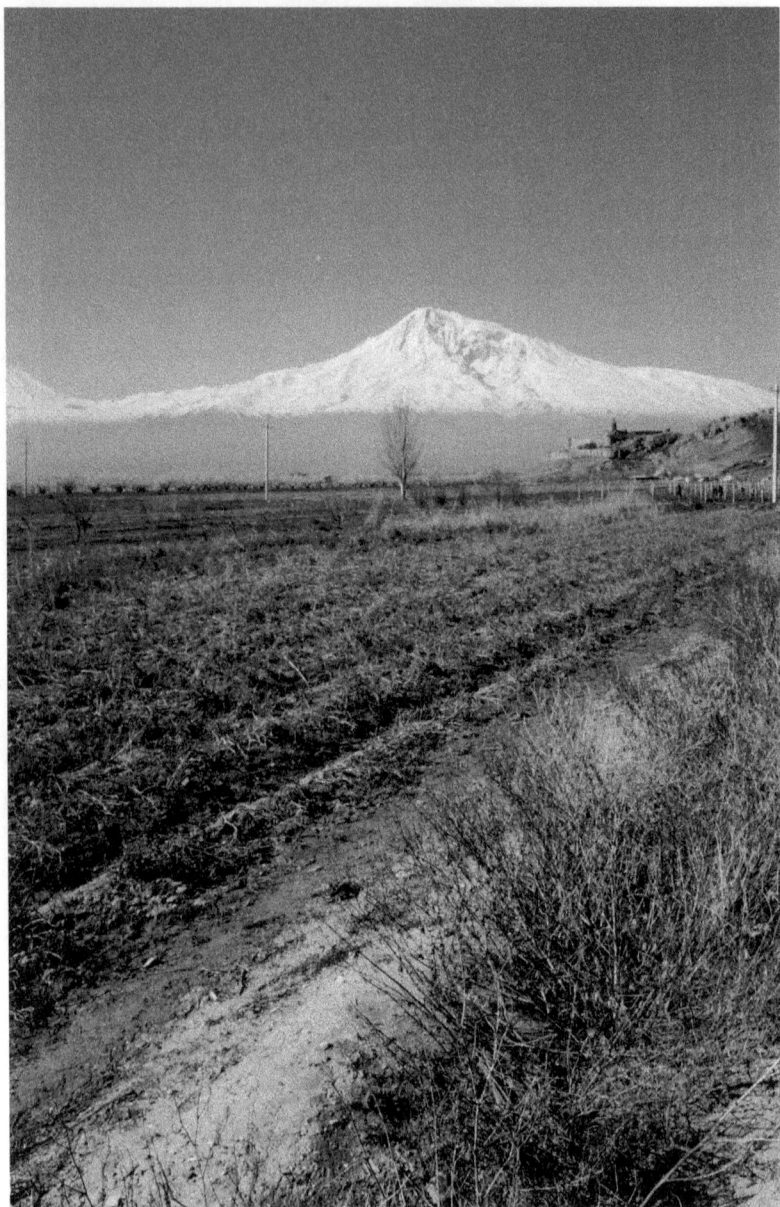

The Armenian monastery, Khor Virap, with Mount Ararat in the background

Chapter 6: Georgia

'Sadness is but a wall between two gardens'
(Goethe, *The Sorrows of Young Werther*)

God gave Georgians wine

A love assignment

I WAS ON MY way to visit a friend called Anton. His mother had assigned me a task to deliver him a small package. I had been driven across the snow-capped Caucasus from Vladikavkaz in Russia by a one-armed taxi driver who stopped occasionally to chew on *churchkhela* – long beads of chewy walnuts soaked in concentrated grape juice. The hotel owner in Tbilisi called it 'Georgian Snickers'. I spotted my taxi driver's handicap immediately, but every other bus and taxi driver turned me down once they saw my passport. Travelers from 'unfriendly countries' were being held for hours at the Russian border and patience did not seem to be the virtue of the sweating, pot-bellied taxi drivers that circled in the heat of the airport car park.

My driver drove as if there were a demon on our tail. If there was a blind corner on a narrow mountain pass, he would floor the accelerator. My Russian co-passenger sitting in the front crossed herself every few minutes as the amputee bore us around a series of switchback turns. Occasionally, she would lean over her shoulder, touch me on the hand and say: *Stiven, vy ochen smelniy* 'Stephen, you are very brave'. Ludmilla did this journey once every few months from Moscow to visit her son who had fled the Russian draft. She was one of a large community of Russian mothers who would go off on these maternal pilgrimages, suitcases packed to the brim with small gifts and snacks for their exiled sons. I grinned, tried not to look over the precipitous edge in search of our predecessors and spent most of the time trying to work out if Georgians drive on the left or the right. The answer to the question was less than obvious.

In Tbilisi, I felt like a lost pilgrim looking in vain for a miracle working icon. I stumbled across the sixth century Anchiskhati Basilica. The door was ajar. Shards of late afternoon light shone on the simple iconostasis in

136

the otherwise dark church. The spectacle reminded me of those descriptions of what a human soul sees when existence begins to flicker, and then it leaves the body. I step into the silence, this house of mysteries, and shut out the world of noise behind me. The whispering of sacred syllables; the breath of God and the tallying up of sins; the lure of that impalpable, spiritual world. The building belongs to an era of Byzantine names so ancient they have almost disappeared from our collective memory – Iberian kingdoms, Persian empires and Bagrationi dynasties. A battle-scarred church, the basilica is a patchwork of chaotic reconstruction, repeatedly destroyed by Turks and Persians and then converted to a museum in the Soviet era. Apart from an appointment with the sacred, the other reason I visited the basilica was to hear the men's vocal ensemble – the soul of Georgia. I watch the five bearded, sturdy looking men – they could easily have been brothers – stand in a line before us and begin to sing. They are dressed in *chokha* and wear a stern expression as if speaking of transgressions. Remarkable polyphonies of longing and mournful cries echo around the basilica (and perhaps right across the mountains of this tiny, ancient land). Souls swoon. There is an uninterruptible calm.

A few head-scarved ladies and me – a refugee from the secular world – stand transfixed, our thoughts having floated somewhere else on the back of these rhythmic melodies. The appeal is cosmic.

The singing has finished and the small huddle begins to stir from the meditative peace. Outside, – another world entirely – dogs snooze in the shade. I have dinner with Anton in a courtyard lined with apricot trees. A Russian exile, he is one of the hordes that seek temporary refuge amidst the trilingual graffiti denouncing Putin. We were living again in ideological times and he was but a remittance man. We dine on all my favorite iconic Georgian dishes – *pkhali, satsivi, ajapsandali* and boat-shaped *khachapuri*. 'Georgia is a vegan's dream, a place of Dionysian oblivion', Anton tells me. And then we work our way through the wine list. A hot wind collected the clouds. The pollen from the capital's maple trees sends me into a paroxysm of sneezing. My first allergy. I nose the *Kisi*, the *Mtsvane*, the *Krakhuna* and the *Manavi*. Would I ever remember the names of any of these wines? Not on the next morning at least:

'Dry before sweet; young before old; modest before fine', says Anton as he assembles the glasses. I can see this is going to be quite an evening. He holds approvingly the glass up to the light.

Anton and I talk about how I have spent the last few days – spurning the cable cars and climbing up the steep hills that encircle Tbilisi in the soaring heat to visit more ancient churches, the guardians of the city. Some of them hung onto cliff edges and served as prisons during the Russian Empire. Beneath, traffic piled up along the embankment of the slate grey Kura which snakes through the city. Or taking refuge from the heat under the Chinese cypress trees that top another one of the hills in the Botanical Garden; photographing the graffiti covered back streets of Tbilisi where vines grow in peoples' yards and carpets hang over balconies. Pomegranate and walnut trees spill over crumbling walls in the steep back alleys. Even if the graffiti's content is expletive, the decorative, flowing Georgian script full of enticing loops appears as poetry to a naïve linguaphile like me. Memory wars and literary purges; plaques to gunned down intelligentsia. The city was remodeling itself entirely. Everywhere I went, buildings were draped with Ukrainian and EU flags and Parisian style *bouquinistes* sold copies of *Mein Kampf*. There was a pre-revolutionary air to the place; an odd conflation of ideologies; a geo-political crossroads – tradition and modernity, East and West. Do we turn left or right? It was perhaps one of those liminal spaces where the new rubs shoulders with the distinctively old.

Anton is a writer and over dinner we discuss the poetic works of exiles and get drunk on culture. There is a melancholy in his voice; his heart miserable. He looks as if the burden of the world rests on his shoulders. He has left behind an unrequited love in Moscow and there is no chance of him returning. It is cruel how history repeats itself with these boundaries of grief. To make matters worse, his closest friend, Vasily, is in love with the same woman. The story has all the ingredients of an epic and shares a number of parallels with Georgia's national epic poem – *The Knight in Panther's Skin* by Rustaveli. Georgians have been reading the poem for eight hundred years; a copy is to be found in more or less every household and it is held to be the coronation of the Georgian national consciousness. I try to cheer him up by reminding him that exiles invariably produce the best work: Nabokov, Zweig, Hugo, Thomas Mann, Brecht, Musil, D. H. Lawrence, Wilde and Kundera. The list was endless:

'It is hopeless, Tatiana is never going to leave him'; 'I'll never get back to Moscow'; 'I must start my life over again'; 'I cannot risk my friendship with Vasily'.

A shadow passed over his face. He knitted his brow, but spoke without rancor for Anton was the kind that would not hurt a fly. Everyone thought a lot of Anton, but not everyone pitied his long run of women problems which had become a standing joke for some. He needed compassion, not pity.

CHAPTER 6: GEORGIA

We order more *Kisi* – its bouquet soft and harmonious –and I try to move the conversation along as we eye up the next course: dried apricots, figs, dates, walnuts – this is a remarkably fertile land. 'Georgia is a Silk Road of flavors', grins Anton as he dives into the medley of local produce:
'Have you seen the street art in Tbilisi?', he asks as he chews on a fig. Tbilisi has become the world's canvass for social commentary. Before I can reply, 'you need to see the Trump/Putin mural'. Not far from the Bridge of Peace, there is a mural of Trump and Putin playing chess whilst sipping on Georgian wine. 'Chess? Surely, the perfect metaphor for our times', I suggest. Then, I remember. I had passed the mural in a taxi this morning. That image lingers over my mind. Putin is one piece ahead but his glass is less full than Trump's.

I sip the *Kisi* – pear flavors mixed in with almond blossom. Then there is the chilling anthropocenic mural depicting the death by poachers of the last white rhino on 18.03.2018. The caption next to the horn that the poachers have cut off reads simply: 'Who is next...?'. Further afield, vast murals covering the side of Soviet apartment blocks portray scenes from medieval Georgian poetry: the son of King Saridan waging war in the valleys of retribution to earn the favor of his beloved who unbeknown to him has already been promised to a princely suitor. Some are more contemporary and provocative. Opposite the Russian Embassy, there is an enormous mural of a young Ukrainian woman holding a bouquet of wild flowers and wearing a subtle, but confident smile. Others depict ancient legends in a retro-futuristic style.

A short pause in our conversation is filled with the heated rhetoric of neighboring diners discussing the situation. We are surrounded by people who speak different languages, air different thoughts and subscribe to different values. Time for a digestif, I feel. I order two shots of *chacha*. Seventy percent proof. A slice of lemon, and then I'll be ready for bed. But our waiter has other ideas, 'three rounds because of Holy Trinity', he grins. I look Anton in the eye and add a small toast: *za drouzba* 'to friendship':
'Many families distil their own *chacha*', says Anton. This particular *chacha* comes from Kakheti in western Georgia. It is made by fermenting grape pomace and then distilling it via water or steam. Traditionally, *chacha* production has been the domain of farmers (not *vignerons*) and the craft is passed down from generation to generation.

As we get up to leave, I espy a priest walking swiftly down the lane. A bottle of *Mtsvane* peeks out from under his vestments. It was the kind of image that I wanted to reconstruct in my mind. 'Well, God gave Georgians wine', I think to myself and amble back to the hotel.

The following days were sultry. The city was ablaze with sunlight. More than once, I sought the shade of the mulberry tree and the refreshment of a homemade lemonade. I would be joined by the stray dogs everywhere I went. All are tagged, harmless and well-fed. Dogs are to Tbilisi what cats are to Istanbul. They sit and wait patiently at pedestrian crossings, get on and off buses. Some even have their own Facebook pages. In the heat of the summer, they spend their days sleeping on the pavements. Then, I would get up and continue my walking tour of Tbilisi only to discover a troupe of stray dogs had been following me. Mile after mile, they would shepherd me round the back streets of the capital as if they were my tourist guides. Tails wagging all the time, they just seem to enjoy the company.

Despite the odious heat, I continued to climb the hills to explore the fringes of the city and the infinities of the mind. The sound of faraway traffic punctuates the distance. My eyes travel up the steep hillsides lighting on ancient fortresses and caravan routes. I receive the occasional message from Anton. The flame of sorrow continues to burn:

'I know Tatiana wants to be with me, but she can't take the step'; 'I am the imprisoned one in exile, but she will not come to visit'; 'God only knows how this situation makes me miserable'.

I respond with, 'What do you say to a little *Kisi* this evening?' Poor Anton was broken-hearted and needed bucking up, I could tell. Later on that day, we sit in quiet, unprepossessing wine bar.

I cast about in my mind to find some words that might console him. 'Anton, I have no doubt that your heart will be healed, that you will find a love that does not rejoice at wrongdoing and that all this sorrow will be turned to joy', I tell him in a sermonic manner:

'Well, I spoke to Vasily this afternoon. We have sworn loyalty to one another. So, it is for her to decide', he said in his normal gentle voice which never rose to anger.

Just at that moment, I remembered the small package which Anton's mother had given me. It had been in my pocket all this time and I had completely forgotten to give it to Anton!:

'Oh, heavens, Anton! I just remembered. Strewth!', arms waving around trying to make sense of my oversight. 'Your mother asked me to give you this. A few letters from home, I think. I am so sorry. It completely passed me by'. It pained me to think how I could have overlooked my mission.

His eyes fix on the package. He unwraps it hastily and a bundle of letters tightly secured with a pink bow falls out. One, two, three, four, five…there are thirteen in total. All addressed to 'my darling, Anton' and sealed with small red stickers in the shape of hearts. On the back was written the name Tatiana Federova.

He sat stock-still for a moment, flushed and then clasped his hands tightly together. A contented smile spread across his face.

Generous tears filled Anton's eyes, but there was to be no riot of emotions. I summon over the waiter. 'Sir, a bottle of your finest *Kisi* please'.

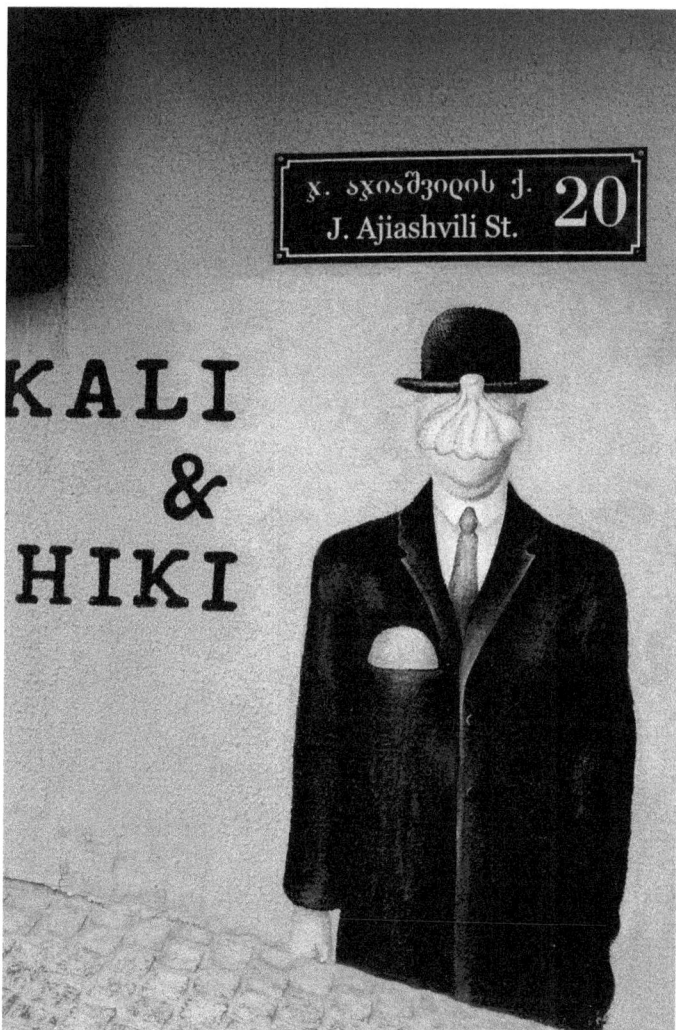

Street art in Tbilisi, Georgia

Chapter 7: Uzbekistan

'Through the clouds of smoke I seemed to see all old Asia before me, and the adventures of past years behind me. A carnival of old camp-scenes danced before my mind's eye, expiring like shooting stars in the night – merry songs which came to an end among other mountains and the dying sound of strings and flutes' (Sven Hedin)

I too am returning from Samarkand

The men and women of Samarkand live in separate worlds

I TOO AM RETURNING from Samarkand, travel-worn and dizzy with new sensations. Spellbound by all that is alien to me, I have been busy embracing the snares of the restless mind. My memory comprises men wearing black flat caps, wads of cash in their back pockets, whispering to one another in *chaikhanas* without menus, but with canaries singing love songs. It is winter and we are sitting outside. How do the canaries survive?

There is only one dish (*plov*) and the clients are mostly secret police. The host decides who and who does not enter his 'restaurant'. His restaurant is his home. The owner of my hotel had organized for me to come here. I was told repeatedly they serve the best *plov* in Samarkand – no finer honor can be bestowed on an Uzbek restaurateur. The taxi driver gave up trying to find the place. I got out of the car and started to ask passers-by for directions in broken Russian. A huddle of men soon formed around me exchanging conflicting information on the whereabouts of my destination. Eventually, I found it hidden away at the end of a narrow lane on the outskirts of Samarkand.

I am eating on the terrace. Small bottles of vodka; warm savory doughnuts with meat are shared; a large dish placed on the center of the table contains the distinctive ochre-colored *plov*. There are only men here, men who smoke endlessly and discuss their code of virtues. One of them, wrapped in brocade, expatiates in halting Russian about the joys of trigamy.

The men and women of Samarkand live in separate worlds.

My memory also comprises Soviet nostalgia; *zhigulis* basking in the sunshine each day; a surreal blue sky; arabesques; the remains of Soviet collective farms; heavenly *shashlik*; hospitality, warmth and kindness on the lips of strangers – none of whom own Smartphones.

Samarkand is cloaked in fresh snow. It is Christmas Day. The pandemic has just come to an end and the streets are empty. It feels like a dream from another era; the glory of a forgotten time even if I know I am seeing only shards of her original splendor. I am no longer living in the moment and thus my holistic vision shines brighter. For how many centuries have traders been coming here poring over the vicissitudes of their travels? You can't forget the city because you have already seen it in your dreams a thousand times. Everything sticks in the mind: its antiquity, the spices of each color in the spectrum; the headwear of a hundred different ethnic groups; the smiling faces of the elderly men who switch between Tajik, Uzbek and Russian; the mosaics; the bearded vultures circling above the markets; the Jewish cemetery where tens of thousands sleep; the light at dusk over Registan. The history and greatness of it all. The Athens and Rome of Central Asia; then throw in the odd camel for the sake of Prokudin-Gorsky.

By the way, it is the morning of Christmas Day. Did I mention it? People are sleeping, or perhaps praying. Seized by the nostalgia of ancient cultures, I meander through obscure empires and Sogdian trade routes. All those trade routes brought religious tolerance. Centuries of tyrants on their caravans, but for the sake of trade there was a need to understand one another. Alexander the Great, Genghis Khan, Ibn Battuta. Who else traveled the caravan routes and came here? Smugglers of elegies brought with them a cargo of sorrows and then all those ruthless warriors that became gardeners. The mystery and metaphysics of attraction leak into the late morning.

I spend days visiting the tombs of the Mongol kings. The romanticizing traveler already knows the city is a carousel of dreams, but he still comes because he wants to forget which century he is in. The spirit finds nourishment here because he can see all that has gone before him. Everywhere the traveler goes, mulberry trees are weighed down by mynah birds which form murmurations at dusk around the madrasahs. They talk and ridicule the traveler, trying to entice him into the shops selling bric-à-brac.

Here, they celebrate the dead. Samarkand is a city of yurt-shaped mausoleums where Islamic mystics, Persian poets and interpreters of dreams are remembered. It was once ruled by astronomers and turbaned men who described the heavens. There was Ulugh Beg and his obliquity of the ecliptic. A man with an ego? He built his own mausoleum.

Sunset, and men migrate from mosque to *chaikhana*. There are discussions to be had; weddings to organize for their teenage daughters.

Otherwise, there is no news from this place, but for centuries it was this spot on the map that mattered. I walk again the unchartered streets or what I like to believe are unchartered streets. Does Samarkand still exist? Or is it just that nothing exists beyond it? The centuries are dead and buried. Its memories defy chronology.

I like to come to places where I don't know which words to speak. There are nations where not only do you not know which words to speak, but you can't read peoples' gazes either. We have though our senses and Samarkand smelt of vanilla.

Elderly men wearing *tubeteika* caps sit around drinking tea and talking of God's mercy and infinity. There are occasional power cuts. Lights flicker, and then darkness. The men look upwards seeking some kind of confirmation of their suspicions and then the conversation continues. The *plov* is replenished; shot glasses are refilled.

At dusk, the birds already roosted, I climb the hill behind the Shah-i-Zinda necropolis in the last possibilities of light and look out across the graveyards. Cupolas pierce the sky. The rugged mountain landscape far in the distance belongs to the Zoroastrian poets. A moment of reflection; the *isha* calls out over Samarkand marking the end of the day as the sky gathers up the darkness. Worship regiments everything here.

* * *

I wake up in Bukhara – the might of Islamic faith – to the sound of finches. The intoxicating touch of freedom urges me out of my hotel bed. I draw the curtains and watch the supernatural slowness of the snow falling. The visceral excitement of discovering a new city means that breakfast is hurried.

Soon, I am exploring with kindled imagination cobblestone backstreets and sun-baked brick minarets before trespassing across the last Emir of Bukhara's summer palace. A Russian glass-fronted refrigerator whence he sated his gluttony is on display. The city is remarkable for its original impulses are intact; the unvanquished that freshly emerge musk-perfumed from an ancient Persian epic poem. The last Emir was nicknamed the Butcher and lived up to his name: a British soldier, Stoddart, came to deliver him a letter stating that the British Empire had no intention of invading his kingdom. Believed to be a spy, the Emir had him thrown into 'the Bug Pit'. He spent three years there in the company of scorpions, rats and sheep ticks. A fellow solider, Connolly, had been sent to negotiate his release. The Emir threw him into the Pit as well. A year later, they were both executed in front of the Ark Fortress. Such stories of uncompromising brutality defined the place. For centuries, almost no Westerner came here, terrified by its dynasties of egos and principalities of assassins. Those that did typically came in disguise and always at peril for their lives. Nowadays, the traveler comes to eavesdrop on a nostalgia for these ancient places of folk memory.

What stays with me most though are the humble memories. The old men shielded in prayers receding into their own wrinkles; the tender salutations of the children that play in the squares flanked with madrasahs decorated with mosaics; a mother clad in traditional dress who walks the Bukhara streets in the evening with her daughters. One of the daughters wishes me 'merry Christmas'. The young Uzbeks like to try out their English. She invites me to walk with her sister and mother. At home during the day, cooking, cleaning and praying – the evening is time for the women to get some fresh air.

The men and women of Bukhara live in separate worlds.

The women are drawn to the stranger. They put me on an esteemed pedestal, but I know I am not worthy of their praise. Habiba has an Arab face, hazel/green eyes, gentle expression and an easy smile. She is respectful, but not obsequious. She apologizes for talking too much, but my mind is busy exploring the cadence of her voice. It is silky like balm, and absolutely flat in terms of intonation. Habiba expects perhaps the man to lead the conversation, but I am not very forthcoming this evening. She takes pains to explain to me the history of the city as we pass the main attractions. The party seems happy doing endless circuits, savoring the familiar dignity of the flow of life. After a few laps, I fabricate a poorly thought-out excuse and repair to the hotel under the glow of the minaret.

As soon as I step into the hotel courtyard, the phone starts bleeping: 'it was honor meeting you'; 'you handsome man'; 'me want you be friend' etc. I thank her for the guided tour. An invitation to dinner the following evening soon ensues.

* * *

Centuries old mulberry trees spread their shadows over the ancient, pre-Islamic back streets. I imagine unverifiable Sufi intrigues, wild trails of sensational conspiracies, accusations of genocide and the like. Labyrinthine, pot-holed and unlit, these passages were made for the spies during the Great Game. In the fading light, men dressed in black *chapans* navigate the narrow alleys with the aid of small, hand-held torches. If it sounds ominous, it isn't. As they pass, they raise their right hand to the heart and greet the stranger with the traditional greeting *salaam alaikum*.

Habiba and her sister escort me through the alleys. Cats scatter before the torchlight. The path to their home seems implausibly circuitous. Finally, a few sharp turns and we enter a tiny courtyard of apricot trees. Boots removed, I am beckoned into a very modest room. Bin liners serve as curtains. There is a very low table adorned with soft drinks and a flat TV screen. Otherwise, the room is empty. We sit on the floor. They kneel effortlessly for long periods of time. I struggle to conceal the soles of my feet and fidget uncomfortably.

They tell me time and time again how honored they are that I accepted their invitation. I am humbled by their kindness. They offer everything to the foreigner. The sister and mother sit glued to the Uzbek dubbed Turkish soap opera. Habiba tells me how she loves English chocolate, but otherwise we talk little. Cadbury's is like gold here. US$20 a bar – almost a monthly salary.

Later in the evening, unable to sit any longer cross-legged on the floor I take my leave and thank my generous hosts. Habiba shows me to the door: 'One day I husband have. I will cook and tell man stories. Until then, I mother's apron strings secured'.

I spend the next hour or so negotiating the labyrinth before making it back to the hotel.

Soon, I will be off again. Trying to avoid the straight road. As always.

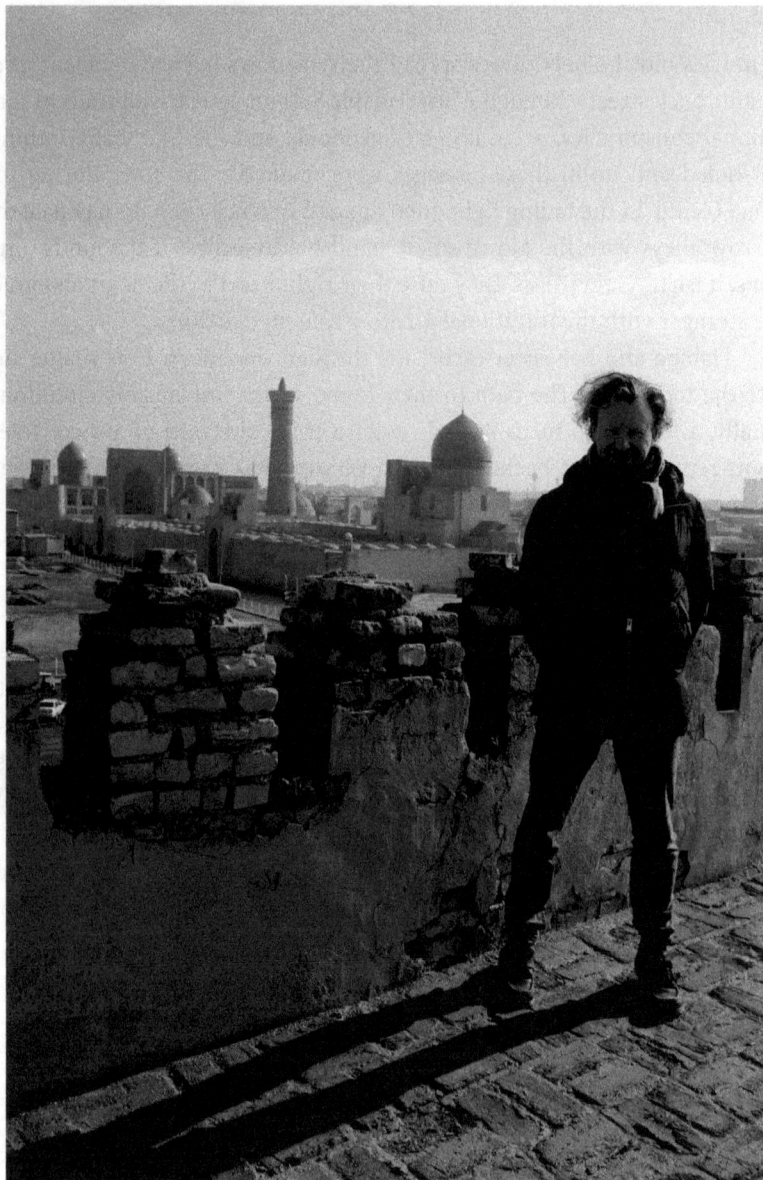

The author in Bukhara

Chapter 8: Greenland

'Silence is the universal refuge, the sequel to all dull discourse and all foolish acts, a balm to our every chagrin, as welcome after satiety as after disappointment' (Henry David Thoreau)

Northumberland Island

Dog-sledding to a remote, uninhabited island in the High Arctic

I AWAKE TO A sallow light. The sky is painted with a few strands of wispy, feathery cirrus cloud in the east. The hardship of the winter is behind me. Hemmed in by solitude and terrorized by four months of darkness in this unforgiving land, I intend now to make the most of my freedom. It is April in the High Arctic and the sunshine cascades into my weather-beaten hut twenty-four hours a day. The season of moonlit ice is over and the regime of time will be of little relevance for the next few months at least. It will only start to get dark again in late August.

There was no real reason for me to travel to Northumberland Island (*Kitiak* in the local language), this uninhabited island in north-west Greenland to where I am headed. It is just there, staring at me in the far distance on those cloud-free days when you can see for a hundred miles. Most of the time it is hidden in a haze of speculation. Remote, and frequently visited by polar bears, it is a place where walruses forage from sea ice platforms and arctic hares pair off to their mating territories. For me, the fact that it was an island, a place on a map was good enough reason to go there. But I also felt as if it might be an adventure that would obey the coordinates of some kind of predestined journey. Something more than just *vagabondage*.

Planning such journeys in my mind, I spent the dark period (*kapir-daq*) from late October to mid-February training my mini dog team of three (*nukka*, *mihka* and *nanoq*). Two bitches (*nukka* and *mihka*) and a dog (*nanoq*). Twice a day, head-torch flashing, I walked around the settlement with a two-meter whip practicing commands *aulaitsit* ('sit'), *harru* ('left'), *atsuk* ('right'), *nuiliqaa-nauk* ('don't get tangled up'), *ai ai ai ai* ('stop') before returning them to the shore ice where they were tethered and fed walrus or seal meat. Leaning over a bucket, I would cut the bloody meat into smallish chunks and toss it to the dogs in turns. The dogs swallow the meat whole, keeping their eye on me all the time. The Inuit were bemused by a *kadluna* ('a white European') training a dog team using Polar Eskimo commands and methods. Traveling by dog-sledge is still the most effective means of travel on the sea ice for them and a large dog team of fifteen strong, well-fed dogs is a reflection of a skilled, successful hunter, but the tradition is normally the preserve of the Inuit.

For some years, I had wanted to have my own dog team and travel in the footsteps of the British explorer, Wally Herbert, who had been the inspiration for my year in the High Arctic. He had lived exactly as the In-ugguit (the name of the Inuit that live in this part of the Arctic) did and learnt all the survival skills he needed from local hunters before attempting to cross the Arctic Ocean. Living in north-west Greenland, I had soon set about learning the art of dog-sledging by going on hunts with the Inugguit to each corner of the frozen Murchison Sound. But for an outsider to have his own dog-team was no straightforward task. No *inuk* would want dogs owned by a *kadluna*. These are not pets, but semi-wild working dogs and the Inuit treat them as tools. A hunter has to rule with absolute authority over his dogs. A few missteps and the whole dog team, heavy sledge and hunter fall through the thin grey ice to a quick death. The Inuit cannot swim. They are reluctant to talk to outsiders about them, but such accidents happen each year.

If I were to have my own dog team, what was I to do when I left the Arctic? For Ibbi, a close hunter friend, the answer was easy. He would shoot them. As that would have been the only foreseeable outcome, I put together instead my own mini-team of hunters' *retired* dogs. Together, the four of us were never going to set any speed records let alone hunt sea mammals, but we would at least be traveling the old ways.

During the dark period, Venus and the moon had shone like a torch on the sea ice. In February, the sun started to set below the horizon. The sunless sky became a rich carmine color for much of the day. Once the darkness started to recede, a whole new frozen world was unwrapped for me and the possibilities seemed endless. I was drawn inexorably to the ice. The appeal of this silent world was spiritual; my internal landscape merged with the unimpeachable authority of the external landscape in an all-em-bracing vision. I had been searching for something greater than myself, a corner of the world that had not yet been rationalized. For the Inugguit, this terrestrial space was *hila* ('consciousness, mind, but also climate and local cosmos'). What it yielded to the eye was more than a panoramic view, it was an extension of the human psyche. The polar desert of the tundra and the sea ice invited a kind of solitude that could be filled with the consciousness and grandeur of these spaces. The sense of place and adventure that arose from it was so stimulating, the thought of loneliness never entered my mind. I loved the simplicity of life in the Arctic, the attempts at harnessing the land and sea for sustenance and the satisfaction of self-reliance. Simple daily chores (smashing up the ice in order to have water to make tea, picking saxifrage to make the tea herbal, collecting the oil for the heater) had become essential liturgies. I was living slowly again.

The Arctic brought everything down to the core: when you are nothing but a tiny, insignificant pin on the frozen sea, the contours of life stare back at you from your long shadow cast in the low April sun. You need to survive and you will only do so if you correctly interpret what surrounds you, what you have become part of (*hila*). After a discussion about *hila*, I once asked an *inuk* in north-west Greenland why he chose to become a hunter. After a long silence, he responded with one word: *ihumanahor-hamahunga* 'I wanted my mind to be open to thinking'. There is beauty in a landscape which solicits this mental freedom, this clarity of perspective gained from standing on top of the world.

Northumberland Island aside, I had construed the edge of the sea ice as my true destiny. I imagined this frozen corridor, the Murchison Sound, tapering to infinity, continuing beyond the icebergs that wobble in the haze in the unquantifiable distance. I felt like a flat-earther with my wish that the ice would continue *ad infinitum*. And, so I had to undertake this journey, to travel to the edge, to see if there was an edge at all and to see what was there on the boundaries of the human psyche.

The sledge has been packed and repacked rather obsessively: fuel cannisters, oil heater, shovel, frozen halibut, walrus and seal meat, *tooq* ('a wooden pole with a pointed edge, a bit like a harpoon but used for testing the thickness of the ice'), *inguriq* ('a reindeer skin to sleep on'), rifle, *pituqqamavit* ('spikes screwed into the ice when the dogs are tethered'), binoculars, satellite phone with solar powered batteries, thermos, kettle, tea and chocolate etc. We will soon be ready for off. The sledge is ready, waiting with the dogs on the broken-up shore ice. I leave my hut perched at the top of the slope and walk down to my mini dog-team. Sleeping dogs stir as I walk past, trying to assess the chances that I might have food for them. Down by the shore, a small crowd is gathered to see me off. Their faces are all framed in my mind now as if that moment is paused and photographed in my memory. They know better than anybody how capricious and fatal the Arctic can be.

I keep the dogs tethered individually and use a triangular fan formation with *nanoq* as the lead dog (*ittuqut*). The two bitches never undermine his leadership. *Nanoq*, nine years old now, can still pull an 80kg weight. With a tremendous amount of fur on his head, *nanoq* (the name means 'polar bear') is very bear like. The leads are attached to their harnesses and through a toggle carved out of walrus tusk are connected to a single rope which pulls the twelve-foot sledge. There is only one way to put a harness on a snarling, excitable male Greenlandic Dog. Every time I did it, I had Nukappianguaq's voice in my head: 'hold the dog's head firmly between your legs with his back between your legs and then try and work out in which hole the dog's head and legs go'. Nukappianguaq who had taught me the art of dog sledging told me he had never seen somebody get it right first time. I was no exception. This, and learning to use the very long whip with precision were what Nukappianguaq and I worked on most in the dark period. Raven-haired and with kind walnut-colored eyes, Nukappianguaq cracked the whip with great expertise, the long whip unfurling just a few centimeters above the dogs' heads.

As I unleash the dogs, jealousy boils over and the dogs begin to fight. Scolding the dogs for their rivalry and love interests, I shout orders (*aulaitsit*) to the scrum of snarling fur caught in the spaghetti of leads. I swish the whip an inch or so above their heads, the dogs cower and soon the social hierarchy is reinstated. We need to move fast now before the fighting begins again. I walk in front of the dogs, holding the whip, and shouting *hak-hak* ('get going'). The dogs follow me. As they head towards the flat ice, there is the normal chaos and mayhem: high-pitched feverish excitement, growling, jostling for position and wagging of tails. I grab onto the stanchions of the sledge, leaning back as far as I can to ensure the dogs do not shoot down the hummocky shore ice. Negotiating the ridges is difficult and even with a small dog team can go badly wrong. I thrash the whip to the side of the dogs, shouting orders, *harru, harru, atsuk, atsuk* navigating them around the hummocks. Once we get onto the flat sea ice beyond the shore, the dogs suddenly accelerate and I have a split second to launch myself onto the sledge. The dogs are so strong, it is no longer possible at this point to stop them by leaning onto the stanchions. For this split-second, there are three options: time your leap right and launch yourself onto the sledge, let go and watch your dog team disappear into the distance or worst of all miss your window, hold onto the sledge and be dragged along the sea ice behind it. Thankfully, this time it went to plan and I gave those on the shore line scrutinizing my preparations little reason to gossip. We all know that I am an amateur at this game.

Fettered with anguish for so long, the dogs are at last set free. I too feel their excitement, that familiar alloy of fear and elation at being unshackled, let loose in this frigid house of sky. When running a dog team, everything is done on the move. The dogs soon get thirsty. They deftly drop their tongue to one side of their jaws and eat the snow as they run along the ice. There is the occasional extremely rapid semi-squat, a response to the excitement. The particles from the excrement's steam freeze instantly forming chandeliers of crystals that become wedged in my beard.

Hak-hak, hak-hak, I settle the dogs into a rhythm and navigate using the icebergs. I head towards a *maniilaq* ('a large, high iceberg with columns') that sits prominently in front of the settlement. The conditions are very good. There is a generous layer of new snow on the sea ice (*matsak*) protecting the dogs' paws from the sharp ice crystals (*pukak*) underneath. A slight wind from the north corrugates the surface snow on the sea ice. It is -27 degrees.

The jagged, angular mountain tops of Herbert Island which lies closer to the mainland than Northumberland grope the sky. The sky is first pink, and then the soft orange light of the early morning sun. The mountain ridges have an unusual sharpness as the folds catch and collaborate with the light. Ahead of us lie statues of ice leaning like drunks on lampposts made of antique glacial water. The dogs are running well and we push on at a steady pace keeping clear of the thin ice around these icebergs. I read the wind from the *aijupinak* ('striae or thin grooves') on the ice. The snow has been largely smoothed over here by the *nigeq* which blows from the east in March and April. I scan the sea ice for polar bear tracks (*tumi*) or evidence of any other kind of life. There are long trails of raven footprints etched into the ice like a secret hieroglyphic code. Expertly camouflaged ptarmigans explode from the snow. Ravens and ptarmigans are the only birds to overwinter in this part of the Arctic.

After about two and half hours of following sledge tracks, we reach a trail of enormous pinnacled icebergs parked in the slow current zone running westwards from Qaanaaq; their transit through the Murchison Sound halted until the summer months. Their edges and grooves shine and glisten in the morning sunshine. These frozen guardians of the Polar North stare down at the solitary dog-sledge and grin at our toil. The silence is very nearly absolute.

I measure our breaks by the icebergs and decide that we will stop when we reach the smallest, flat-topped tabular iceberg (*natsinnarraaq*) resembling a monumental frozen coffee table. It turns out this particular iceberg is colossal. It just appears small because it is so far away. An hour later and we have still not passed it. Some of the icebergs we are passing are like mountain ranges or ancient turreted, frozen castles locked in the ice. It is almost impossible to guess the height of the icebergs as there is nothing to compare them with, but I would guess that some of these might be one hundred meters high. In the Arctic, there are icebergs nearly the height of the Eiffel Tower.

We travel close to Herbert Island (not in fact named after Wally Herbert) and I see what appears to be the abandoned settlement where he lived in the 1970s. The light is constantly playing with my mind, flashing me tantalizing distorted images of weather-beaten houses floating in the sky: the optical pitfalls of the Arctic. The rays of the sun bend and twist – a polar Fata Morgana. Distorting and confusing, the island is suddenly without fixed definition. Now that my eyelashes are partially glued together with *kaniq* ('the frost that forms on eye lashes'), I am not sure I can trust my own eyes. Perfectly adapted to the cold, the Inugguit with the tiniest of eyelashes do not have this problem. Passing the settlement, I am reminded of the story where Wally Herbert was gone for weeks hunting. His young wife became worried and begged the Inugguit to go and look for him. They refused. They thought Wally would be ashamed if he knew the Inugguit were searching for him. Shortly after, he returned to the settlement safely after a successful hunting trip.

ai, ai, ai, ai, I shout to the dogs. We stop for a rest. I listen to the crooning wind and stamp my feet to restore circulation. I thaw my eyelashes over a mug of steaming tea. The dogs lie in the sun, their protruded noses sniffing the wind. I watch the *natserivik* ('the snow that blows across the surface of the sea ice') create, reshape and then erase mesmerizing patterns on the ice. Within a few weeks, this frozen highway will suddenly transform: the ice around the western tip of Herbert Island will become thin because of the *aukarneq*, the fast current that runs around the peninsula; leads will begin to appear in the ice indicating the movement of walruses underneath, glaucous gulls will congregate on the sea ice. The island's slopes will come alive with the arrival of coalitions of squabbling sea birds. With melted eyelashes, I see through the binoculars what are indeed the abandoned houses of Herbert Island ripped to pieces by storms: shaky wooden frames with their polar bear fur insulation exposed. This settlement was an active community up until the 1990s, but is now a jumble of memories that swirl in the wind.

We have been traveling already for six hours and keen to maintain the pace, we continue on our journey. I walk in front of the dogs, whip in hand, and then hop onto the sledge that darts past me. Beyond the largest icebergs, the smooth sheet of sea ice turns subsequently into a major ice rubble field (*maniidat*) reflecting the strong current underneath; a chaotic frozen jumble of broken ice stretching for about two nautical miles. Instead of practically skating along, the dogs now clamber over sheets of collided, fractured ice jutting up about five feet high. I jump off and push the sledge from behind, leaning with all my weight against the stanchions. The sledge groans and creaks as it is thrown at obtuse angles. The next hour or so is spent fighting our way through a polar obstacle course. There is much cursing, but we manage not to flip the sledge and to get beyond the rubble field and back onto the flat ice.

Our journey continues for nearly ten hours under the halo of the brilliant sun. The sound of the sledge runners bumping rhythmically across the frozen sea is soporific. Exhausted from pushing the heavy sledge over the rubble field, my head begins to dip. Fortunately, my legs are a bit too long for the sledge. They keep sliding off the wooden platform, jabbing into the hard sea ice under the moving sledge, reminding me that I should not doze. A hunter I used to visit in Savissivik (a settlement of forty people) lost his leg to frostbite after falling asleep on his sledge. Over tea, he rolled up his trouser to reveal a wooden leg. On the sea ice, he woke up to find his dogs had stopped pulling and fallen asleep. His right leg was frozen solid. My dozing is only properly interrupted once we pass through the insidious evening shadow of Herbert Island. Out of the sun, the temperature plummets suddenly ten degrees and it becomes desperately cold. The moisture from my breath freezes on my face. My eyelashes begin to freeze together again impairing my vision. Practically anaesthetized on the sledge, I force myself to hop off every ten minutes or so and jog behind, holding onto the uprights and trying to keep the blood circulating to my feet which now feel like lumps of wood.

The size of Herbert Island seems almost mythical, constantly deceiving me, throwing up rock formations which look like the tip of the island only to reveal themselves as another gully. By early evening, we pass Herbert Island and turn the corner into Ikerasak, the channel that runs between Herbert and Northumberland Island. Now facing Northumberland Island, the evening sun in the western sky is still shining bright. Tonight (April 12), we will have the first midnight sun of the year. Just two months ago, there was no sun at all. Qaanaaq is now out of view. The dogs and I are now totally alone out here. It feels as if we are traveling to a borderless mythical place, the end of the world, in search of the elusive ice edge.

Shortly after ten in the evening, we arrive at what the local hunters call flippantly the *hotelli*. The dogs clamber up a steep slope and there at the foot of a mountain is a tiny, gingerbread colored hut which Nukapiannguaq built in the 1980s. The roof is meringued with snow. There is a network of huts around this part of the Arctic. Many have been damaged or blown away in storms, but thanks to four massive boulders attached to the roof with ropes, this one is still standing. Arriving at camp, the first thing to do is feed the dogs. In preparing for the trip, Nukapiannguaq invited me to use his *qingnivik* ('a subterranean meat store'). This is a food cache under the ice where hunters store meat. When hunting polar bear, hunters are away for weeks at a time and cannot carry all the meat that they need. The *qingnivik* is an outdoor freezer; a hole covered with a large slab of ice which polar bears are unable to move. As the temperature is below zero for much of the year, meat can be stored here for many months at a time. Using my *tooq* as a lever, I prize open the lid to the *qingnivik* and grab a frozen leg of walrus meat.

I shovel away the snow that has drifted against the entrance of the cabin and open the door with the polar bear proof handle (to open, push up not down). I curse at the rubbish left behind by the previous occupants, but quickly clean everything up. Then, I suspend the frozen lump of walrus meat over the brass Primus paraffin pressure stove using a pulley system conveniently installed in the hut. The meat slowly thaws. I feed the dogs. Armed with binoculars and a rifle, I go for a short walk to see if there are signs of polar bears. Tonight, for the first time during my stay in the High Arctic, this feels like a real possibility. It is nearly midnight. Wisps of snow skitter in the distance. The sky is empty. I stand, enveloped in inviolable silence. There are different types of silences, but this silence is an unforgettable one: a harmonious feeling of being alone, but being party to something bigger than myself. I am content to have finally set foot on, what is for me at least, my Arctic Nowhere. I have withdrawn from this world, and for a short while bask in the silence and solitude as an abstract spectator.

I stroll back to the cabin. The crunching sound my boots make as I walk on virgin snow echoes around the place. Everything seems to echo, both past and present. Even if it seems I am alone with the dogs, as I walk up the slope I can see there is evidence of other life here. Delicate, oval shaped tracks of the arctic fox criss-cross the snow. By the time I get back to the hut, the dogs are curled up, sleeping in tight balls of tan, copper and sepia. My bed for the night is a reindeer skin on a hard, uncomfortable wooden sleeping platform (*i'ddeq*). I fall asleep to the sound of dripping walrus meat. It is nearly midnight and the sunshine floods the cabin.

I awake in this fortress of constant, sempiternal light. It feels like I am sitting under a spotlight. The day is about to begin. The heater is still warbling and the hut remained warm overnight. I peel back the reindeer skins, prepare some porridge for breakfast and check on the dogs. In absolute silence, they sit on the look-out. Everything is glossy and precise. With a lighter sledge, we will be traveling further east today towards the edge of the sea ice. With the sledge repacked, we travel for about two hours before coming close to the end of Northumberland Island. Hakluyt Island (*Apparhuit*) is visible in the distance, but is surrounded by open water. Just beyond the Kissel glacier, I stop the dogs (*ai ai ai...*) to test the ice with the *tooq*. There are grey patches and the pole soon goes through the ice. Clouds of smoke (*pujoq*), the shape of ogees, above the water in the distance tell me that we are near open water (*imaq*). The sea steam is like a laundry room. This so-called 'sea smoke' occurs when still cold air overruns the warm, moist air at the sea surface. Leaving the dogs on the ice, I head to land and climb up to a vantage point, binoculars around neck and rifle slung over shoulder. Ahead, the ice is thin with patches of open water between major ice rubble fields. The recent full moon must have resulted in a lunar spring tide which has broken up the ice. The sea ice that forms during neap tides is normally firm and smooth. That is when the Inuit hunt walrus. There will be no neat, clean distinction between ice and open water, as I imagined. I will not be tiptoeing up to the edge of this white world and looking out onto a pale blue sea. There are no edges, clear boundaries or black and white certainty about what lies beyond.

With the binoculars, I scan the smashed-up ice. Bathymetric maps begin to wobble. It squeaks and creaks like an old rusty door, indicating that it is thin and dangerous. The dogs can smell something. Their nostrils are flared and they are looking east. In the distance, I can hear a deep grunting noise. I look in that direction with the binoculars, but see nothing. Then I spot a walrus lying on an ice floe next to some freshly broken ice. It is a male, and the grunting noise is its mating call. I sit down in the snow and through the binoculars watch this giant mound of blubber and hide wobble on the ice. He awkwardly drags his bulk across the ice floe, just to flop into the water and then climb slowly back up again. Close to where I left the dog team, I spot some *nakkut*, narrow leads in the ice which have frozen over again, and possible indications of the path of the walrus moving underneath towards land. There must be other walruses around, but I cannot see any. Satisfied that we can go no further, I rejoin the dog team and we travel along the edge of the rubble field to see if there is any other sign of life before heading back to the hut.

Once at the cabin, I climb up the slope to the look-out-point. I spot a sledge way in the distance: an almost indistinguishable speck on the silvery mantle. Iggiannguaq, a hunter who lives in my settlement, turns up at the hut two hours later wearing polar bear trousers and a caribou skin anorak (*qulittaq*). He has a kind, gentle face. His pleated wrinkles smile at me, forming a network of narrow channels and tributaries meandering between low banks of skin across his forehead. Shortly after he arrives, he digs up a large slab of meat from the deep subterranean refrigerator. In a hail of crude jokes, he soon joins me in the hut. Over a pot of boiled walrus and blubber, Iggiannguaq – a born conspirator – tells me about his views on life *hamani* 'down there' (by which he means 'the rest of the world'). Never having set foot in a town, let alone a city, he shakes his head and says *ajorpoq* ('bad'), 'too many people'. He talks to me about how the doctrines of *hila* determine the course of the day, the consciousness and mind and how nature's delicate pleasures make you content, fulfilling the poverty of your inner life.

We talk, pour tea and watch through the window the wind re-upholster the sea ice. Anxious to escape the stifling heat of the hut, I cut up the thawed seal meat and go and feed the dogs. I push open the heavy door. Cold air billows into the cabin. Smelling the blood and guts slopping around in the buckets, the dogs bark and howl; the normal feeding-time pandemonium ensues. Their cries and songs escalate into a crescendo that circles around the island. It is only after feeding time and during the worst weather that the dogs are completely silent. Later in the evening, their baying resembles a form of evening communion to which I fall asleep. Throughout my time in the Arctic, the dogs were like an eclectic fellowship of saints and sinners whose personalities shaped every event. I take a short evening walk and return to the hut to find Iggiannguaq snoring under his reindeer skins.

I spend the night at the cabin and awake to lavender northern skies. I repack the sledge and make the preparations to head back to Qaanaaq. Shortly before I am about to head off, Nukappiangguaq calls me on the satellite phone. He wants me to bring back some meat from the *qingnivik* for his dog team. I load up the sledge with slabs of frozen walrus. I say goodbye to Iggiannguaq who sits in the cabin, sharpening his knives. He hugs me and says *nanngmanniartutin aggurruaq* ('make sure you look after yourself'). There are tears in his eyes.

On the way back, I see polar bear tracks that lead from Herbert Island northwards across the Murchison Sound. The tracks are fresh and clearly defined, but no sign of a bear. The journey back to Qaanaaq seems never-ending at times and the dogs are tired pulling our swollen load. When we arrive in late evening, it is as if we never left. A group of hunters are on the shore ice, sharing jokes whilst repairing a sledge. As I approach the settlement, the men start to clap. One of them bellows: *piniartoq nuutaq* ('the new hunter'). Everybody laughs. I talk with the hunters about Northumberland Island and then feed the dogs. I produce the frozen walrus meat from Nukappiangguaq's *qingnivik* and tell them what a successful hunting trip I have had. *Hunaa…*('oh, gosh…'), one of them shouts and then they roll around laughing. I walk up the slope to my hut. My house is cool, but not freezing. The oil heater belches and splutters as it always does when the tank is low. I refill the tank just in time and the room starts slowly to warm up. I am exhausted and get straight into my sleeping bag. I peep through the frustratingly thin curtains. The sun circles above me in a sky without contrails, before twisting into a rictus of anguish. Then, the phone rings. Immediately, I recognize the voice that speaks to me in slow, creaky Polar Eskimo:

> 'Stiffi, it is Iggianuguaq. The broken ice has been all blown away. I am at the ice edge now. There is just the deep blue sea and I can hear the walruses talking. You should come back, my friend. There is time. We wait for you.'

www.ingramcontent.com/pod-product-compliance
Lightning Source LLC
Chambersburg PA
CBHW062223080426

42734CB00010B/2001